# THE
# CAT FANATIC

# THE
# CAT
# FANATIC

## Quirky Quotes on
## Frisky Felines

**Edited by Charles Elliott**

JR
BOOKS

First published in Great Britain in 2007 by JR Books, 10 Greenland Street,
London NW1 0ND

Introduction and text order copyright © 2000 Charles Elliott

The contents of *The Cat Fanatic* are drawn from *The Quotable Cat Lover.*

A catalogue record for this book is available from the British Library.

ISBN 978 1 906217 00 6

1 3 5 7 9 10 8 6 4 2

Designed by Nancy Freeborn, FreebornDesign

Printed by CPI Bookmarque, Croydon, England

To Kate and Maggie

# CONTENTS

# INTRODUCTION

Judging from the amount of thought devoted over the centuries to figuring out what goes through their furry little heads, it is probably safe to say that cats fascinate more human beings than do any other member of the animal kingdom, with the possible exception of dogs, horses, and other human beings. People become fixated on cats. They turn into cat people. They think about their cats, talk obsessively about their cats, worry about their cats—and write about them. There is, consequently, a vast literature of cats, much of it unspeakably sentimental. In compiling a collection of cat quotes, therefore, the first duty is to harden one's heart.

While I cannot pretend to have succeeded in absolutely every case (I invite you to discover the one quote in this book that, in retrospect, seems to me to fall just beyond the pale) I have tried to limit myself here only to those writings and sayings about cats made memorable by their seriousness, humor, perceptiveness, or ingenuity. Fortunately, there are plenty of these. An unexpectedly wide range of writers famous for other subjects turn out to have been cat people (or sometimes cat haters, but there's room for them too), and plucking quotes out of their books has been a real pleasure. Then there are the two or three cat books that are themselves classics. I think particularly of Carl Van Vechten's *The Tiger in the House*, now nearly eighty years old but still probably the best literary cat book, meaning a book that approaches cats via literature and vice versa. Van Vechten, a best-selling novelist and chronicler of Jazz Age Harlem who is now virtually forgotten, was obviously obsessed by both cats and books.

Anyone who produces a book about cats, even in the tangential way I have done here, is generally expected to offer references as to his qualifications as a cat lover. This often consists of a long scroll of thanks to his own cats, who are listed by name. Now I do like cats; we have two—Sam and Rosie—and they both amuse and occasionally exasperate our household. But as Sidney Denham notes in his bibliography of cat books, *Cats Between Covers*, "Other people's stories about their cats can be as tedious as stories about their children," so I'll spare you. In any case, in my experience, while the average cat is fully capable of threatening the Sèvres on the mantelpiece, scattering bits of mouse on the living room rug, terrorizing neighborhood dogs, and making use of the favorite geranium pot as a public convenience, one thing he's not, ever, is boring.

# THE
# CAT FANATIC

BEHAVIOUR

Anyone who has lived on terms of comparative equality with a cat knows that he will show his intelligence fifty times a day. To be sure this intelligence is usually of the variety called selfish.

—CARL VAN VECHTEN
***THE TIGER IN THE HOUSE*** (1921)

Cats can obviously rise to considerable mental heights, at least when they want to satisfy their lower instincts.

—AKIF PIRINÇCI AND ROLF DEGEN
*CAT SENSE* (1994)

Cats are rather delicate creatures
and they are subject to a good many
different ailments, but I never heard
of one who suffered from insomnia.

—JOSEPH WOOD KRUTCH
*THE TWELVE SEASONS* (1949)

Cat said, "I am not a friend, and I am not a servant. I am the Cat who walks by himself."

—RUDYARD KIPLING

*JUST SO STORIES* (1902)

Kipling's cat . . . probably never thought he was walking alone. On the contrary, he may have thought he was walking with Kipling and . . . trying to lead the author out of the wet, wild woods.

—ELIZABETH MARSHALL THOMAS
*THE TRIBE OF THE TIGER* (1994)

It is a very inconvenient habit of kittens . . . that, whatever you say to them, they always purr.

—LEWIS CARROLL
*THROUGH THE LOOKING GLASS
AND WHAT ALICE FOUND THERE*
(1871)

Cats invented self-esteem.

—ERMA BOMBECK (1927–1996)

All cats were at first wild, but were at length tamed by the industry of Mankind; it is a Beast of prey, even the tame one, more especially the wild, it being in the opinion of many nothing but a diminutive Lyon.

—WILLIAM SALMON
*THE COMPLEAT ENGLISH PHYSICIAN OR THE DRUGGIST'S SHOP OPENED* (1693)

Pussy . . . symbolically gives a twist of a yawn, and a lick to her whiskers. Now she proceeds to clean herself all over, having a just sense of the demands of her elegant person,— beginning judiciously with her paws, and fetching amazing tongues at her hind-hips. Anon, she scratches her neck with a foot of rapid delight; leaning her head towards it, and shutting her eyes, half to accomodate the action of the skin, and half to enjoy the luxury. She then rewards her paws with a few more touches; look at the action of her head and neck, how pleasing it is, the ears pointed forward,

and the neck gently arching to and fro!
Finally she gives a sneeze, and another
twist of mouth and whiskers, and then,
curling her tail towards her front claws,
settles herself on her hind quarters, in
an attitude of bland meditation.

—LEIGH HUNT

**"THE CAT BY THE FIRE"** *THE SEER,
OR, COMMON-PLACES REFRESHED*
(1840)

The theory of the American Shakers that the functions of sex "belong to a state of nature and are inconsistent with a state of grace" is not held by the cat.

—CARL VAN VECHTEN
*THE TIGER IN THE HOUSE* (1921)

Scratching, petting or rubbing to
a cat is a sign of unending, in fact
unendable, infancy.

—ROGER CARAS
*A CAT IS WATCHING* (1989)

A cat . . . plays for her own enjoyment, in a self-contained way, with no desire to share. Shut her up alone, and a ball, a fringe, or a looped piece of string is enough to make her give herself up to silent and graceful sport. While she is playing she does not say, "Man, I'm so awfully glad I've got you here!" She will play beside the bed of a corpse.

—KAREL ČAPEK
***INTIMATE THINGS*** (1935)

Unfortunately there were no mice in our top floor
flat. . . . Yet she was forced to obey the ancient
laws that none can counter, and hunt mice . . .
She simply took what she could get—in this case
potential mice—Rodent Presences—and became
engrossed by them to the point of addiction.

—JULIA STRACHEY
"BREAKFAST IN PERCY STREET"
QUOTED IN *JULIA: A PORTRAIT BY
HERSELF* BY FRANCES PARTRIDGE
(1983)

The cat is not in the long run anxious to please.

—T. O. BEACHCROFT
*JUST CATS* (1936)

Cats have a sense of humor, as is shown in their extreme love of play. A middle-aged cat will often play as unreservedly as a kitten, though he knows perfectly well it is only a game.

—WILLIAM LYON PHELPS (1865–1943)

The cat, which is a solitary beast, is single minded and goes its way alone, but, the dog, like his master, is confused in his mind.

—H. G. WELLS (1866–1946)

If the cat waits for long hours, silent beside
the crack of the wainscot, it is for pure pleasure.
Cats do not keep the mice away; it is my belief
that they preserve them for the chase.

—OSWALD BARRON (1868-1939)

Movement is terribly important to a cat . . .
Nothing works quite so well as an object of
jumpable size moving away. For cats, that
is virtually impossible to resist.

—ROGER CARAS
*A CAT IS WATCHING* (1989)

If you say "Hallelujah" to a cat,
it will excite no fixed set of fibres
in connection with any other set
and the cat will exhibit none of the
phenomena of consciousness. But if
you say "Me-e-at," the cat will be
there in a moment, for the due
connection between the sets of
fibres has been established.

—SAMUEL BUTLER
*THE NOTEBOOKS OF SAMUEL BUTLER* (1912)

Cats seem to go on the principle that it never does any harm
to ask for what you want.

—JOSEPH WOOD KRUTCH

*THE TWELVE SEASONS* (1949)

The cat cleans her face
with a look of delight.

—JOHN CLARE (1793–1864)

Macavity, Macavity, there's no one like Macavity

There never was a Cat of such deceitfulness and

    suavity,

He always has an alibi, and one or two to spare:

At whatever time the deed took place

    MACAVITY WASN'T THERE!

—T. S. ELIOT
"MACAVITY THE MYSTERY CAT"
IN *OLD POSSUM'S BOOK OF
PRACTICAL CATS* (1939)

After witnessing a cat's wedding,
no young novelist can rest content
with the falsehoods and banalities
which pass, in current fiction, for
descriptions of love.

—ALDOUS HUXLEY
**"SERMONS IN CATS" IN** *MUSIC*
*AT NIGHT* **(1931)**

Confront a cat with something he has never seen before and his first reaction will almost invariably be one not of fear but of curiosity.

—MICHAEL JOSEPH
*CAT'S COMPANY* (1930)

She [his cat Taki] has another curious trick (which may or may not be rare) of never killing anything . . . Mice bore her, but she catches them if they insist and then I have to kill them.

—RAYMOND CHANDLER

IN A LETTER QUOTED IN *THE WORLD OF RAYMOND CHANDLER* EDITED BY MIRIAM GROSS (1977)

Cat sentimentality is a human thing. Cats

are indifferent, their minds can't comprehend

the concept "I shall die," they just go on living.

> —GAVIN EWART
> "SONNET: CAT LOGIC" IN
> *THE COLLECTED EWART 1933-80*
> (1980)

Oh Major is a fine cat
He walks cleverly
And what is he at,
my fine cat?
No one can see.

—STEVIE SMITH

**"MY CAT MAJOR" IN** *THE COLLECTED POEMS OF STEVIE SMITH* **(1975)**

Cats have a consuming passion for watching human beings.

—AKIF PIRINÇCI AND ROLF DEGEN
*CAT SENSE* (1994)

Why did not fate make our breasts proof against the wild play of calamitous passion? O Appetite, thy name is cat!

—E. T. A. HOFFMANN
*LEBENSANSICHTEN DES KATER MURR* (1923 EDITION)

If cats have been the friends of man for so many centuries, could nature not have adapted itself, just a little, away from the formula: five or six kittens to the litter, four times a year?

—DORIS LESSING
*PARTICULARLY CATS* (1967)

What female heart can gold despise?
What cat's averse to fish?

—THOMAS GRAY
**"ODE ON THE DEATH OF A**
**FAVOURITE CAT, DROWNED IN**
**A TUB OF GOLDFISHES"** [1748]
*POEMS* (1778)

A cat knows how to anticipate.

—ROGER CARAS
*A CAT IS WATCHING* (1989)

The cat lives alone. He has no need of society. He obeys only when he wishes, he pretends to sleep the better to see, and scratches everything he can scratch.

—FRANÇOIS RENÉ, VICOMTE DE CHATEAUBRIAND (1768–1848)

A Cat is a familiar and well known beast . . . Ovid saith, that when the Giants warred with the Gods, the Gods put upon them the shapes of Beasts, and the sister of Apollo lay for a spy in the likeness of a Cat, for a Cat is a watchful and wary beast seldome overtaken, and most attendant to her sport and prey.

—EDWARD TOPSELL
*THE HISTORIE OF FOUR-FOOTED BEASTES* (1607)

Most cats, when they are Out want to be In, and vice versa, and often simultaneously.

—LOUIS J. CAMUTI AND
LLOYD ALEXANDER
*PARK AVENUE VET* (1962)

The reason domestic
pets are so lovable
and so helpful to us
is because they enjoy,
quietly and placidly,
the present moment.

—ARTHUR SCHOPENHAUER
**QUOTED BY AGNES REPPLIER IN**
*THE FIRESIDE SPHINX* (1901)

A cat is not merely diverted by everything that moves, but is convinced that all nature is occupied exclusively with catering to her diversion.

—FRANÇOIS AUGUSTE PARADIS DE MONCRIF

QUOTED BY AGNES REPPLIER IN *THE FIRESIDE SPHINX* (1901)

"Gentlemen, I used to have a cat here, by the name of Tom Quartz, which you'd 'a' took an interest in, I reckon—most anybody would. I had him here eight year—and he was the remarkablest cat I ever see. He was a large grey one of the Tom specie, an' he had more hard natchral sense than any man in this camp—'n' a power of dignity—he wouldn't let the Govner of Californy be familiar with him. He never ketched a rat in his life—'peared above it. He never cared for nothing but mining."

—MARK TWAIN
**"DICK BAKER'S CAT" IN**
***ROUGHING IT* (1872)**

"I'm not one o' those as can see the cat i' the dairy, an' wonder what she's come after."

—GEORGE ELIOT
*ADAM BEDE* (1859)

Cats are autocrats of naked self-interest.

—CAMILLE PAGLIA
*SEXUAL PERSONAE* (1990)

People like pets to possess the same qualities they do. Cats are irresponsible and recognize no authority, yet are completely dependent on others for their material needs. Cats cannot be made to do anything useful. Cats are mean for the fun of it. In fact, cats possess so many of the same qualities as people that it is often hard to tell the people and the cats apart.

—P. J. O'ROURKE (1946– )

Cats, no less liquid than their shadows,

Offer no angles to the wind.

They slip, diminished, neat, through loopholes

Less than themselves.

—A. J. TESSIMOND
*CATS* (1934)

Thrice the brindled cat hath mewed.

—WILLIAM SHAKESPEARE
*MACBETH* (1623)

Everyone acquainted with the cat knows that he is as capable of disinterested affection and gratitude as any so-called gregarious animal—the wolf and the jackal, let us say, and their not very nice relation, the domestic dog.

—W. H. HUDSON
*STRAND MAGAZINE* (1922)

Now it is very common with young cats, and not at all rare with old cats of the common and persian breeds . . . when comfortably lying on a warm shawl or other soft substance, to pound it quietly and alternately with their fore-feet; their toes being spread out and claws slightly protruded, precisely as when sucking their mother. . . . This curious movement is commonly excited only in association with the sensation of a warm soft surface; but I have seen an old cat, when pleased by having its back scratched, pounding the air in the same manner; so that this act has almost become the expression of a pleasurable sensation.

—CHARLES DARWIN
*EXPRESSION OF THE EMOTIONS IN MAN AND ANIMALS* (1872)

A tail held straight out behind a cat means that the cat is about to attack, say the experts. If it is expressing itself loudly in cat language at the same time, it means you have shut its tail in the door.

—JOHN TICKNER
*TICKNER'S CATS* (1987)

"Mice, Kitchener, mice! Go seek!" cried my mother, who had no real vocation for cats.

—SYLVIA TOWNSEND WARNER
"MY FATHER, MY MOTHER, THE BENTLEYS, THE POODLE, LORD KITCHENER, AND THE MOUSE" IN *SCENES OF CHILDHOOD AND OTHER STORIES* (1981)

A dog is like a liberal. He wants to please everybody. A cat really doesn't need to know that everybody loves him.

—WILLIAM KUNSTLER
**IN *ESQUIRE* (1971)**

The cat, if you but singe her tabby skin,

The chimney keeps, and sits content within:

But once grown sleek, will from her corner run,

Sport with her tail, and wanton in the sun:

She licks her fair round face, and frisks abroad

To show her fur, and to be catterwaw'd.

—ALEXANDER POPE

"THE WIFE OF BATH, HER
PROLOGUE" TRANSLATED
FROM CHAUCER'S *CANTERBURY
TALES* (1714)

The more you rub a cat
on the rump, the higher she
sets her tail.

—JOHN RAY

*A COLLECTION OF ENGLISH
PROVERBS* (1670)

A cat can be trusted to purr when she is pleased, which is more than can be said for human beings.

—WILLIAM RALPH INGE
*A RUSTIC MORALIST* (1934)

Walking is a human habit into which dogs readily fall but it is a distasteful form of exercise to a cat unless he has a purpose in view.

—CARL VAN VECHTEN
**QUOTED IN *PLAIN AND FANCY CATS*
EDITED BY JOHN BEECROFT (1958)**

A Cat is much delighted to play with hir image in a glasse, and if at any time she behold it in water, presently she leapeth down into the water which naturally she doth abhorre, but if she be not quickly pulled forth and dryed she dieth thereof, because she is impatient of all wet.

—EDWARD TOPSELL
*THE HISTORIE OF FOUR-FOOTED BEASTES* (1607)

If a dog jumps up into your lap, it is because he is fond of you; but if a cat does the same thing, it is because your lap is warmer.

—ALFRED NORTH WHITEHEAD
**DIALOGUES OF ALFRED NORTH WHITEHEAD (1977)**

The world is like a cat thrown into a river to drown; it has pulled itself out somehow or other, and is at the moment cleaning itself up, buffing its fur with its tongue.

—BENJAMIN CONSTANT

IN A LETTER TO MADAME DE
NASSAU, DECEMBER 31, 1831

WATCHING
CATS

Everyone who owns
a cat is a cat-watcher.

—ROGER CARAS
*A CAT IS WATCHING* (1989)

Very few human beings are privileged to know the cat. He does not care whether you like him or not. . . . He is a philosopher of independent spiritual means.

—MICHAEL JOSEPH
*CAT'S COMPANY* (1930)

The cats are well. We call Podge the
Air Raid Warden. She comes dashing
in the moment the sirens go. Polly
has to be called, and Podge, in shelter,
watches anxiously for her arrival.
Podge, from the start, has taken aero-
planes seriously, and while anything is
overhead, lies with her eyes anxiously
looking up at the ceiling.

—ARTHUR RANSOME
**LETTER TO HIS MOTHER,
15 SEPTEMBER 1940, QUOTED IN
*THE LIFE OF ARTHUR RANSOME*
BY HUGH BROGAN (1984)**

Visited Edward Evans in the dark hole in the hovel roof which does duty for a bedroom, and a gaunt black and white ghostly cat was stalking about looking as if she were only waiting for the sick man to die, that she might begin upon him.

—FRANCIS KILVERT [1874]
*KILVERT'S DIARY* EDITED BY
WILLIAM PLOMER (1947)

What astonished him was that cats should have two holes cut in their coats exactly at the places their eyes were.

—GEORG CHRISTOPH LICHTENBERG
*REFLECTIONS* (1799)

A kitten can

Bite with his feet;

Papa and Mamma

Have more teeth.

—THEODORE ROETHKE
"WHERE KNOCK IS OPEN WIDE" IN
*COLLECTED POEMS* (1966)

A grey old cat his whiskers licked beside;

A type of sadness in the house of pride.

—GEORGE CRABBE
THE PARISH REGISTER (1807)

The domestic cat is a contradiction. No animal has developed such an intimate relationship with mankind, while at the same time demanding and getting such independence of movement and action.

—DESMOND MORRIS
*CATWATCHING* (1986)

Fat rear haunches

   toes, tail,

   half a mouse

      at the door at dawn.

      Our loving cat.

—GARY SNYDER
"I:VI:40077" *AXE HANDLES* (1983)

One dry slim paw, like that of a black rabbit, threatened the heavens; and a tiny kitten spotted like a civet cat, slumbering replete and prostrate on its back in the middle of this disorder, looked as though it had been assassinated . . .

—COLETTE
*MY MOTHER'S HOUSE* (1922)

I love in the cat that independent and almost ungrateful temper which prevents him from attaching himself to anyone; the indifference with which he passes from the salon to the housetop.

—FRANÇOIS RENÉ,
VICOMTE DE CHATEAUBRIAND
**QUOTED BY COMTE DE MARCELLUS
IN *CHATEAUBRIAND ET SON TEMPS*
(1859)**

It is needless to spend any time over her loving nature to man, how she flattereth by rubbing her skin against one's legs, how she whurleth with her voice, having as many tunes as turnes, for she hath one voice to beg and to complain, another to testify her delight and pleasure, another among her own kind by flattering, by hissing, by puffing, by spitting, in so much as some have thought that they have a peculiar intelligible language among themselves.

—EDWARD TOPSELL
*THE HISTORIE OF FOUR-FOOTED
BEASTES* (1607)

I saw my cat undecided in its mind whether he should get up on the table and steal the remains of my dinner or not. The chair was some eighteen inches away, with its back towards the table, so it was a little troublesome for him to get his feet first on the bar and then on the table. He was not at all hungry but he tried, saw it would not be quite easy and gave it up; then he thought

better of it and tried again,
and saw again that it was not all
perfectly plain sailing; and so
backwards and forwards with
the first-he-would-and-then-he-
wouldn'tism of a mind so nearly
in equilibrium that a hair's
weight would turn the scale
one way or the other.

—SAMUEL BUTLER

*THE NOTEBOOKS OF SAMUEL BUTLER* (1912)

There was something theatrical and grandiloquent about him, and he seemed to pose like an actor who attracts admiration. His motions were slow, undulating, and full of majesty; he seemed always to be stepping on a table covered with china ornaments and Venetian glass, so circumspectly did he select the place where he put down his foot.

—THEOPHILE GAUTIER
**ON HIS CAT ENJOLRAS**
***MÉNAGERIE INTIME* (1869)**

I have just been given a very engaging Persian kitten . . . and his opinion is that I have been given to him.

—EVELYN UNDERHILL (1875–1941)

I wish I knew as much about natural history and the habits of animals as Calvin does. He is the closest observer I ever saw; and there are few species of animals on the place that he has not analyzed. I think he has, to use a euphemism very applicable to him, got outside of every one of them, except the toad.

—CHARLES DUDLEY WARNER

*MY SUMMER IN A GARDEN* (1870)

The cat is the only non-gregarious domestic animal. It is retained by its extraordinary adhesion to the comforts of the house in which it is reared.

—FRANCIS GALTON
*INQUIRIES INTO HUMAN FACULTY*
(1883)

Do you see that kitten chasing so prettily her own tail? If you could look with her eyes, you might see her surrounded with hundreds of figures performing complex dramas, with tragic and comic issues, long conversations, many characters, many ups and downs of fate.

—RALPH WALDO EMERSON
*EXPERIENCE* (1841)

When cats run home and light is come
And dew is cold upon the ground.

—ALFRED LORD TENNYSON
"THE OWL" IN *THE POEMS
OF TENNYSON* EDITED BY
CHRISTOPHER RICKS (1969)

Every one is aware that a perfectly comfortable, well-fed cat will occasionally come to his house and settle there, deserting a family by whom it is lamented, and to whom it could, if it chose, find its way back with ease. This conduct is a mystery which may lead us to infer that cats form a great secret society, and that they come and go in pursuance of some policy connected with education, or perhaps with witchcraft. We have known a cat to abandon his home for years. Once in six months he would return, and look about him with an air of some contempt. "Such," he seemed to say, "were my humble beginnings."

—ANDREW LANG
"AT THE SIGN OF THE SHIP" IN
*LONGMAN'S MAGAZINE*, MAY 1904

I remember a night in a villa on the Florentine hills, a green Florentine night . . . a dumb curiosity seized two of us and caused us to leave our chairs on the loggia where the faint breeze flickered the flames of the Roman lamps and the tall bottles of golden strega stood half-filled, to mount the stairs, led on by a nameless questioning, and to seek the chamber directly above the spot where we had been sitting, the temporary abode of two white Persian cats. . . . The room was empty when we entered; the bright moonlight streaming in from the doorway which led to a terrace which formed the roof of the loggia told us that. Noiselessly, and apparently unreasonably, we stole carefully across the broad chamber and looked out. . . . I can still see the expression of horror on my companion's face, perhaps reflected on my own, as we stood just hidden by the hangings at the doorway and saw the two cats softly lift their paws from two white doves who rose unsteadily, dizzily, and lazily into the green atmosphere, while the cats rolled on their backs, stretching their claws to the air and making faint mews. . . .

—CARL VAN VECHTEN
*THE TIGER IN THE HOUSE* (1921)

We saw upwards of a million cats in Bermuda, but the people are very abstemious in the matter of dogs. . . . It is a great privilege to visit such a land.

—MARK TWAIN
"THE STOLEN WHITE ELEPHANT" IN *RAMBLING NOTES OF AN IDLE EXCURSION* (1878)

As the cat
climbed over
the top of

the jamcloset
first the right
forefoot

carefully
then the hind
stepped down

into the pit of
the empty
flowerpot

—WILLIAM CARLOS WILLIAMS
**"POTTED CAT" IN *THE COLLECTED
POEMS OF WILLIAM CARLOS
WILLIAMS* (1986)**

A cat is sometimes inaccurately
described as a domesticated animal.
Fundamentally, he is no more
domesticated than a crocodile.

—MICHAEL JOSEPH
*CAT'S COMPANY* (1930)

While rain depends, the pensive cat gives o'er

Her frolics, and pursues her tail no more.

—JONATHAN SWIFT
"A DESCRIPTION OF A CITY
SHOWER" IN *COMPLETE POEMS*
EDITED BY PAT ROGERS (1983)

The cat pretends to sleep that it may see the more clearly.

—FRANÇOIS RENÉ,
    VICOMTE DE CHATEAUBRIAND
    (1768–1848)

All dogs look up to you. All cats look down on you. Only a pig looks at you as an equal.

—ATTRIBUTED TO
WINSTON CHURCHILL (1874–1965)

Peter [the cat] was agreeable. So Tom
pried his mouth open and poured down
the Pain-killer. Peter sprang a couple of
yards in the air, and then delivered a
war-whoop and set off round and round
the room, banging against the furniture,
upsetting flower-pots, and making
general havoc. Next he rose on his hind
feet and pranced around, in a frenzy of
enjoyment, with his head over his
shoulder and his voice proclaiming his
unappeasable happiness. Then he went
tearing around the house again
spreading chaos and destruction in his
path. Aunt Polly entered in time to see
him throw a few double somersets,

deliver a final mighty hurrah, and sail through the open window, carrying him 'thout any more feeling than if he was a human!

—MARK TWAIN
*THE ADVENTURES OF TOM SAWYER*
(1876)

In the cat I see woman with her
ever-changing, sensitive soul.

GIACOMO CASANOVA (1725–1798)

I really am a cat transformed into a woman.

—BRIGITTE BARDOT (1934- )

A small ad in a newspaper once described a lost kitten as answering to the name of "Go Away."

—MARK BRYANT
*THE COMPLETE LEXICAT* (1992)

I cannot honestly report that I have ever seen a feline matron of this class (alley) washing her face when in an interesting condition.

—CHARLES DICKENS (1812–1870)

You remember my ideal cat has always a huge rat in its mouth, just going out of sight—though going out of sight in itself has a peculiar pleasure.

—EMILY DICKINSON
*THE LETTERS OF EMILY DICKINSON*
EDITED BY THOMAS JOHNSON
(1986)

Hawks for sunlight; owls for half-light; but for the night, cats.

—DORIS LESSING
*PARTICULARLY CATS* (1967)

No cat purrs unless
someone is around
to listen.

—ELIZABETH MARSHALL THOMAS
*THE TRIBE OF THE TIGER* (1994)

While I dislike as much as any other cat lover the sight of two cats trying to tear each other to shreds, I must confess to being an enthusiastic fan of tom cat duels. There is, after all, a lot to admire in a mechanism which so effectively minimizes physical injury.

—JEREMY ANGEL
*CATS' KINGDOM* (1985)

a cat mistrusts the sun

keeps out of its way

only where sun and shadow meet

it moves

a horse loves the sun

it basks all day

snorts

and beats its hooves

the sun likes horses

but hates cats

that is why it makes hay

and heats tin roofs.

—ROGER McGOUGH

*SELECTED POEMS 1967-1987* (1989)

Cats are by nature very stubborn and may resist what they learn and already know when it interferes with their essential character as voluptuaries.

—ROGER CARAS
*A CAT IS WATCHING* (1989)

The two cats never fought, physically. They fought great duels with their eyes.

—DORIS LESSING

***PARTICULARLY CATS*** (1967)

Cat properties are like ranches. The space enclosed by the cat's boundaries is actually the grazing land for livestock, whether deer or deer mice, which belong to the owner and no one else, and which the owner does not disturb except to harvest.

—ELIZABETH MARSHALL THOMAS
*THE TRIBE OF THE TIGER* (1994)

Cats virtually always underestimate human intelligence just as we, perhaps, underestimate theirs.

—ROGER CARAS
***A CAT IS WATCHING*** (1989)

There is, incidentally, no way of talking about cats that enables one to come off as a sane person.

—DAN GREENBURG (1936- )

Cats, while animals of prey, are useful as domestics; that while showing wisdom, they have more attachments to places than to people; they have light, adroit, clean and voluptuous bodies; they love ease and search out the softest furniture; they take naps all day long and so repose and rest themselves; they are pretty as young cats and possess a very proper way to amuse children (if the strokes of their paws was not to be feared); they seem to have a natural dread of water, cold and bad smells; they are attracted to perfumes and allow themselves to be caressed by people who wear them; and they have eyes that "imbibe light" by day and give off light at night.

—GEORGES-LOUIS LECLERC,
COMTE DE BUFFON
*HISTOIRE NATURELLE, GÉNÉRALE*
*ET PARTICULIÈRE* **(1749–1788)**

Q: Where does a two-thousand-pound gorilla sleep?

A: Anywhere it wants to.

Q: Where does a ten-pound cat sleep?

A: Anywhere it wants to.

—LEONORE FLEISCHER
*THE CAT'S PYJAMAS* (1982)

The kitten went, or rather hopped, down the stairs, each of which was twice her height: first front paws, then flop with the back; front paws, then flop with the back.

—DORIS LESSING
*PARTICULARLY CATS* (1967)

If there is one thing this town has plenty of, it is kittens, which finally grow up to be cats, and go snooping around ash cans, and mer-owing on roofs, and keeping people from sleeping good.

—**DAMON RUNYON**
"LILLIAN" IN *GUYS AND DOLLS*
(1930)

Obese cats are far less common than obese dogs (or obese people).

—DESMOND MORRIS
*CATLORE* (1987)

Bearing in mind that the figures are only a rough guide, the following table may be of interest. The ages are given in years:

| Your cat's age | Your own age |
|:---:|:---:|
| 1 | 15 |
| 2 | 25 |
| 4 | 40 |
| 7 | 50 |
| 10 | 60 |
| 15 | 75 |
| 20 | 105 |
| 30 | 120 |

—DESMOND MORRIS
*CATLORE* (1987)

Cats and dogs amicably embracing before a grate of glowing coals exist chiefly in the reckless imagination of the greetings card artist, who does nothing for credibility by adding the caption "Good Pals" in flowing script.

—BASIL BOOTHROYD
*LET'S MOVE HOUSE* (1977)

LIVING
TOGETHER

God made the cat to give man the pleasure of stroking a tiger.

—FRANÇOIS-JOSEPH MÉRY
(1798–1865)

Minnow, go to sleep and dream,
  Close your great big eyes;
Round your bed events prepare
  The pleasantest surprise.
Darling Minnow, drop that frown,
  Just cooperate,
Not a kitten shall be drowned
  In the Marxist State.
Joy and Love will both be yours,
  Minnow, don't be glum.
Happy days are coming soon—
  Sleep, and let them come.

—ELIZABETH BISHOP
"LULLABY FOR THE CAT" FROM
THE COMPLETE POEMS
1927-1979 (1983)

A bulletin from Archy the Cockroach, who started out last July to hitch-hike from Hollywood to New York with Mehitabel the Cat and Mehitabel's seven platinum-blonde kittens:

had a great ride boss

got a ride on the running board of a car

and caught up with mehitabel

in new mexico where she is gadding about

with a coyote friend

i asked her where the kittens were

kittens mehitabel said kittens

with a puzzled look on her face

why goodness gracious I seem to remember

that I did have some kittens

I hope nothing terrible has happened

to the poor little things but if something has

I suppose they are better off

an artist like me shouldnt really

have offspring it handicaps her career

archy I want you to meet my boyfriend

cowboy bill the coyote I call him

I am trying to get him to come to new york

with me and do a burlesque turn

isnt he handsome I said tactfully that he looked

very distinguished to me and all bill said

was nerts insect nerts

    archy

      —DON MARQUIS
       *ARCHY'S LIFE OF MEHITABEL* (1933)

It occurs to me that I can't remember ever reading about a murderer who gave house room to, or was fond of, a cat.

—P. D. JAMES

*TIME TO BE IN EARNEST* (1999)

Cats have loving hearts.
But they also have self-respect,
and a tendency to love only
that which is lovable. It is this
trait which their human masters
cannot forgive.

—DOROTHY CANFIELD FISHER
(1879–1958)

Cats . . . appear to regard human beings who may be domiciled with them rather as part of the furniture than as comrades.

—LOUIS ROBINSON
*WILD TRAITS IN TAME ANIMALS*
(1897)

## STRICT, UNBENDING RULES FOR DEALING WITH STRAY CATS

1. Stray cats will not be fed.

2. Stray cats will not be fed anything except dry cat food.

3. Stray cats will not be fed anything except dry cat food moistened with a little milk.

4. Stray cats will not be fed anything except dry cat food moistened with warm milk, yummy treats and leftover fish scraps.

5. Stray cats will not be encouraged to make this house their permanent residence.

6. Stray cats will not be petted, played with, or picked up and cuddled unnecessarily.

7. Stray cats that are petted, played with, picked and cuddled will absolutely not be given a name.

8. Stray cats with or without a name will not be allowed inside the house at any time.

9. Stray cats will not be allowed inside the house except at certain times.

10. Stray cats will not be allowed inside the house except on days ending in "y".

11. Stray cats allowed inside will not be permitted to jump up on or sharpen their claws on the furniture.

12. Stray cats will not be permitted to jump up on, or sharpen their claws on, the best furniture.

13. Stray cats will be permitted on all furniture but must sharpen claws on the new $114.99 sisal-rope cat-scratching post with three perches.

14. Stray cats will answer the call of nature out-doors in the sand.

15. Stray cats will answer the call of nature in the three-piece, high-impact plastic tray filled with Fresh'n'Sweet kitty litter.

16. Stray cats will answer the call of nature in the hooded litter pan with a three-panel privacy screen and plenty of head room.

17. Stray cats will sleep outside.

18. Stray cats will sleep in the garage.

19. Stray cats will sleep in the house.

20. Stray cats will sleep in a cardboard box lined with an old blanket.

21. Stray cats will sleep in the special Kitty-Komfort-Bed with nonallergenic lamb's wool pillow.

22. Stray cats will not be allowed to sleep in our bed.

23. Stray cats will not be allowed to sleep in our bed, except at the foot.

24. Stray cats will not be allowed to sleep in our bed under the covers.

25. Stray cats will not be allowed to sleep in our bed under the covers except at the foot.

26. Stray cats will not play on the desk.

27. Stray cats will not play on the desk near the computer.

28. Stray cats are forbidden to walk on the computer keyboard on the desk when the human is jdvirikacnk9230-kcekmcm,asmjduu USING IT.

—ANON
MESSAGE CIRCULATED
ON THE INTERNET (1998)

Q. We have cats the way most people have mice. [Signed] Mrs. C. L. Footloose.

A. I see you have. I can't tell from your communication whether you wish advice or are just boasting.

—JAMES THURBER
**"THE PET DEPARTMENT" IN**
*THE OWL IN THE ATTIC AND*
*OTHER PERPLEXITIES* (1931)

The cat's asleep; I whisper kitten

Till he stirs a little and begins to purr—

He doesn't wake. Today out on the limb

(The limb he thinks he can't climb down from)

He mewed until I had him in the house.

I climbed up to get him: he mewed.

What he says and what he sees are limited.

My own response is even more constricted.

I think, "It's lucky; what you have is too."

What do you have except—well, me?

I joke about it but it's not a joke:

The house and I are all he remembers.

Next month how will he guess that it is winter

And not just entropy, the universe

Plunging at last into its cold decline?

I cannot think of him without a pang.

Poor rumpled thing, why don't you see

That you are no more, really, than a man?

Men aren't happy. Why are you?

—RANDALL JARRELL
"THE HAPPY CAT" IN
*THE COMPLETE POEMS* (1969)

The cat who lived at the Palace had been awarded the headdress of nobility and was called Lady Myōbu. She was a very pretty cat, and his Majesty saw to it that she was treated with the greatest care.

—SEI SHŌNAGON

*THE PILLOW BOOK* [10TH CENTURY]
**TRANSLATED BY IVAN MORRIS**
**(1967)**

Cats find humans useful domestic animals.

—GEORGE MIKES (1912–1987)

If [in Egypt] a cat dies in a private house by a natural death, all the inmates of the house shave their eyebrows.

—HERODOTUS (c. 480–425 B.C.)
*HISTORY*

The worth of a cat and her teithi [qualities, necessary attributes] is this:

1. The worth of a kitten from the night it is kittened until it shall open its eyes is a legal penny.

2. And from that time, until it shall kill mice, two legal pence.

3. And after it shall kill mice, four legal pence; and so it always remains.

4. Her teithi are, to see, to hear, to kill mice, to have her claws entire, to rear and not to devour her kittens; and if she be bought, and be deficient in any one of those teithi, let one third of her worth be returned.

—HYWEL DDA, PRINCE OF SOUTH WALES CODES ENACTED c. 940

By living both with other cats (its mother and litter-mates) and with humans (the family that has adopted it) during its infancy and kittenhood, it becomes attached to both and considers that it belongs to both species . . . It may be a cat physically, but mentally it is both feline and human.

—DESMOND MORRIS
*CATWATCHING* (1986)

A cat cannot be said to have any politics. Yet it is always polite. In its outlook is the ultimate and final egoism; yet it is always a charming companion.

—T. O. BEACHCROFT
*JUST CATS* (1936)

The cat is for those who care little for
demonstrative affection, and much more
for the subtle intimacies of the spirit.

—FRANK SWINNERTON
*TOKEFIELD PAPERS* (1949)

It is often said that the dog is more intelligent than the cat, because you can teach the former more tricks. The fact is really evidence for the cat. When you command a dog to "sit up," the poor idiot thinks he has to do it. The average cat throws it off, perhaps to be stupid and not understand what you want. He really understands you too well, but he sees "nothing in it" for him. Why sit up?

—WILLIAM LYON PHELPS (1865-1943)

Any relationship
with human beings
other than equality is
impossible for the cat.

—FELIX SALTEN (1869–1945)

Housemate, I can think you still
   Bounding to the window-sill
   Over which I vaguely see
   Your small mound beneath the tree,
   Showing in the autumn shade
   That you moulder where you played.

—THOMAS HARDY
"LAST WORDS TO A DUMB FRIEND"
IN *COLLECTED POEMS* (1930)

The beast was brought in the evening. It didn't make a good impression then, but in the morning, in the full light of day, it looked even worse. It was exorbitantly ugly, that cat. Skinny as a nail, with a long head like a pike and, to add to the picture, black lips; it was an inelegant ash-gray color, and its coat was dull and dry. Its bald tail resembled a string with a tuft on the end, and the fur on its belly, which had doubtlessly been skinned in some accident, dangled like bits of fluff swept up from a carpet. Despite its large caressing eyes, in whose emerald depths swirled flecks of gold, its poverty-stricken and dubious coat marked it as a low son of the gutter, an unacceptable cat. But this unacceptable cat, I accepted, because he showed himself willing to be caressed. I looked after him, and I baptized him with the name "Mouche."

—JORIS-KARL HUYSMANS
INTERVIEW IN *BÊTES ET GENS DES LETTRES* BY GEORGES DOCQUIS (1895)

Frontin wasn't just a cat, he was a poodle for goodness, a camel for sobriety, a monkey for intelligence. In summer, he would follow me on walks through the woods at Romainville; in winter he never left my study. Curled up the whole day long on a cushion next to my desk, he would sleep as long as I worked, as if to avoid bothering me; but when I rose he would rise too, stretching his back and fixing me with his golden eyes as if to say, "Now we can talk, right?" And we did.

—PAUL DE KOCK (1793-1871)

There, taking out of his pocket bones and pieces of meat, he [Ezra Pound] begins to call the cats. He knows all their histories—the brindled cat looked like a skeleton until he began to feed it; that fat grey cat is an hotel proprietor's favourite, it never begs from the guests' tables and it turns cats that do not belong to the hotel out of the garden; this black cat and that black cat fought on the roof of a four-storied house some weeks ago, fell off, a whirling ball of claws and fur, and now avoid each other. Yet now that I recall the scene I think that he has no affection for cats—"some of them so ungrateful", a friend says—he never nurses the café cat, I cannot imagine him with a cat of his own.

—WILLIAM BUTLER YEATS

*A PACKET FOR EZRA POUND* (1929)

But thousands die without or this or that,
Die, and endow a college or a cat.

—ALEXANDER POPE

*MORAL ESSAYS* (1731–1735)

Cats I scorn, who sleek and fat,
Shiver at a Norway Rat;
Rough and hardy, bold and free,
Be the cat that's made for me!

—ERASMUS DARWIN
QUOTED IN *MEMOIRS OF THE LIFE OF DR. DARWIN* BY ANNA SEWARD (1804)

I would be present, aye,
    And at my Ladie's call;
To gard her from the fearful mouse,
    In Parlour and in Hall;
In Kitchen, for his Lyfe,
    He should not shew his head;
The Peare in Poke should lie untoucht
    When shee were gone to Bed.
The Mouse should stand in Feare,
    So should the squeaking Rat;
And this would I do if I were
    Converted to a Cat.

—GEORGE TURBERVILLE
"THE LOVER" IN *EPITAPHES,
EPIGRAMS, SONGS AND SONETS*
(1567)

Some men there are
love not a gaping pig;
Some that are mad if
they behold a cat.

—WILLIAM SHAKESPEARE
*THE MERCHANT OF VENICE* (c. 1597)

It is quite a cheering thought to realize that cats sometimes hate as keenly as people, that they too contrive their little revenges and Sicilian vendettas whereby they may in some small degree compensate for the insults doled out to their race.

—CARL VAN VECHTEN
*THE TIGER IN THE HOUSE* (1921)

You ought to 'ave tom cats arranged, you know—it makes 'em so much more companionable.

—NOEL COWARD
"CAT'S CRADLE" IN *COLLECTED SKETCHES AND LYRICS* (1931)

I have noticed that what cats most appreciate in a human being is not the ability to produce food which they take for granted—but his or her entertainment value.

—GEOFFREY HOUSEHOLD
*ROGUE MALE* (1939)

Let a man get up and say, "Behold, this is the truth," and instantly I perceive a sandy cat filching a piece of fish in the background. Look, you have forgotten the cat, I say.

—VIRGINIA WOOLF
*THE WAVES* (1931)

Many cats, that the Borodins lodged, marched back and forth on the table, thrusting their noses into the plates or leaping on the backs of the guests. . . . Another installed himself on Borodin's shoulders and heated him mercilessly. "Look here, sir, this is too much!" cried Borodin, but the cat never moved.

—NIKOLAI RIMSKY-KORSAKOV
*MA VIE MUSICALE* (1914)

They say the test of [literary power] is whether a man can write an inscription. I say, "Can he name a kitten?" And by this test I am condemned, for I cannot.

—SAMUEL BUTLER

*THE NOTEBOOKS OF SAMUEL BUTLER* (1912)

PS.—I have christened your cat
"Purdoe," a good name for a cat.
I baptized it with ink.

—ELIZA MARY ANNE SAVAGE
LETTER TO SAMUEL BUTLER,
MARCH 10, 1873

The Naming of Cats
is a difficult matter.

—T. S. ELIOT

**"THE NAMING OF CATS" IN**
*OLD POSSUM'S BOOK OF*
*PRACTICAL CATS* **(1939)**

The lack of imagination or invention
most people display in naming pussies
is almost beyond credence.

—CARL VAN VECHTEN
*THE TIGER IN THE HOUSE* (1921)

Other people's stories about their cats can be as tedious as stories about their children.

—SIDNEY DENHAM
*CATS BETWEEN COVERS* (1952)

Cats have always refused to share the human failing of having a conscience.

—JOHN TICKNER
*TICKNER'S CATS* (1987)

My cat is dead
But I have decided not to make a big
tragedy out
   of it.

—WENDY COPE
"AN UNUSUAL CAT POEM" IN
*SERIOUS CONCERNS* (1992)

Pashas love tigers; me, I love cats. Cats are the tigers of poor devils.

—THEOPHILE GAUTIER (1811–1872)

A home without a cat, and a well-fed, well-petted, and properly revered cat, may be a perfect home, perhaps, but how can it prove its title?

—MARK TWAIN

*PUDD'NHEAD WILSON* (1894)

The kitten of whom I told you last year is now a confirmed cat. He is much larger than he seemed likely to become, and is vigorous and vagrant, but not, I am sorry to say, either affectionate or intelligent. It is not known that he ever caught a mouse; he dislikes rain, but has no knowledge of how to avoid it if it falls; and if one caresses him he is very likely to scratch one. He is, however, very proud of his name.

—MAX BEERBOHM

LETTER TO LYTTON STRACHEY ON HIS CAT STRÉ-CHI, QUOTED IN *LYTTON STRACHEY* BY MICHAEL HOLROYD (1967–1968)

Our Office cat is a happy cat
She has two hundred kittens
And every one has been adopted into
happy
    homes
By our cat-loving Britons.

—STEVIE SMITH
  **"OUR OFFICE CAT" IN**
  ***THE COLLECTED POEMS OF***
  ***STEVIE SMITH* (1975)**

Men prefer pets they can control, like dogs. They can't handle that "get stuffed" stare from a cat.

—CELIA HAMMOND

*EVENING STANDARD MAGAZINE,*
MARCH 26, 1999

With one of the most bewitching sounds in the world, its purr, the cat persuades us that it thinks we're wonderful.

—AKIF PIRINÇCI AND ROLF DEGEN
*CAT SENSE* (1994)

A cat has to be in a very bad mood if a human cannot coax him to purr.

—DEREK TANGYE

*A CAT IN THE WINDOW* (1962)

Polly-Hodge still purrs, still grooms herself fastidiously and obviously still enjoys life. When the moment comes when that life is no longer agreeable and it is apparent that she is suffering it will be painlessly ended. We are often more merciful to our animals than we are to each other.

—P. D. JAMES
*TIME TO BE IN EARNEST* (1999)

One may live in a house for six months with a cat and never receive from it a single kindly word or look . . . .Yet, suddenly and without any cause, this very same cat will one day become, for half an hour or an hour, your dearest friend.

—*THE SPECTATOR*,
26 FEBRUARY 1898

I knew that there would be a cat in the house. Just as one knows, if a house is too large people will come and live in it, so certain houses must have cats.

—DORIS LESSING
*PARTICULARLY CATS* (1967)

In truth, most of us don't know our cats.

—ELIZABETH MARSHALL THOMAS
***THE TRIBE OF THE TIGER*** (1994)

The phrase "domesticated cat" is an oxymoron.

—GEORGE F. WILL (1941– )

All cats, given the opportunity,
are people-watchers.

—ROGER CARAS
*A CAT IS WATCHING* (1989)

A cat is the ideal baby surrogate,
a Peter Pan who never grows up and
provides constant satisfaction for
our mothering instincts.

—AKIF PIRINÇCI AND ROLF DEGEN
*CAT SENSE* (1994)

Knowing cats, a lifetime of cats, what is left is a sediment of sorrow quite different from that due to humans: compounded of pain for their helplessness, of guilt on behalf of us all.

—DORIS LESSING
*PARTICULARLY CATS* (1967)

A Boston attorney, Woodbury Rand, bequeathed $40,000 to his pet cat Buster, cutting his relatives off without a penny because of "their cruelty to my cat." Buster died in 1945, intestate.

—LEONORE FLEISCHER
*THE CAT'S PYJAMAS* (1982)

A Poet's Cat, sedate and grave
As poet well could wish to have . . .

—WILLIAM COWPER (1731–1800)

Authors like cats because they are such quiet, lovable, wise creatures, and cats like authors for the same reason.

—ROBERTSON DAVIES
*THE ENTHUSIASMS OF ROBERTSON DAVIES* (1990)

If you want to write,
keep cats.

—ALDOUS HUXLEY (1894–1963)

It is a curious truth that many cats enjoy warmer, more convivial, even affectionate relationships with humans than they could ever do with fellow felines.

—BRUCE FOGLE
*THE CAT'S MIND* (1991)

Anyone who has owned many cats in long succession can define his or her life as a series of furry episodes.

—ROGER CARAS
*A CELEBRATION OF CATS* (1989)

I am certainly not Agrippina's mistress, and the assumption of authority on my part would be a mere empty dignity, like those swelling titles which afford such innocent delight to the Freemasons of our severe republic.

—AGNES REPPLIER

*THE FIRESIDE SPHINX* (1901)

Certain assumptions have to be made when you are dealing with anything as arcane as a cat.

—ROGER CARAS
*A CAT IS WATCHING* (1989)

Domesticated felines remain "part-kitten" all through their lives, and even though they may be middle-aged in feline terms they still look upon their human owners as their mothers.

—DESMOND MORRIS
*CATLORE* (1987)

There was a certain company of Monks much given to nourish and play with Cats, whereby they were so infected, that within a short space none of them were able to say, read, pray, or sing, in all the Monastery.

—EDWARD TOPSELL
*THE HISTORIE OF FOUR-FOOTED BEASTES* (1607)

Only cats are little company. All the dogs have died. Many cats too, but we have two left . . . snakes, thieves, coyotes, even owls; just the desert. It is hard on those soft little things.

—MARIA HUXLEY
**LETTER OF 1945 QUOTED IN
*ALDOUS HUXLEY* BY SYBILLE
BEDFORD (1974)**

Tom Jones [a cat] soon learned that he was welcome to install himself at the very heart of genius on Nabokov's chest, there to make starfish paws, purr ecstatically, and sometimes—rather painfully for the object of his pleasure—knead. I like to imagine that *Lolita* was being dreamed of that year and that Tom Jones's presence may have had something to do with the creation of that sensuous world.

—MAY SARTON
*THE FUR PERSON* (1957) ON HER
CAT AND VLADIMIR NABOKOV,
AUTHOR OF *LOLITA*

I envy you your wife, your home, your child— I was going to say your cat. There would be cats in my home too if I could but get it.

—ROBERT LOUIS STEVENSON

**LETTER TO EDMUND GOSSE IN 1879, QUOTED IN *ROBERT LOUIS STEVENSON* BY FRANK McLYNN (1993)**

Alas old animals are so much nicer; I love my cat now, but it took about 8 years.

—NANCY MITFORD
LETTER TO LADY REDESDALE
DECEMBER 16, 1959 QUOTED IN
*THE OXFORD DICTIONARY OF*
*HUMOUROUS QUOTATIONS* (1995)

I have nothing to say to "charming" women. I feel like a cat among tigers.

—KATHARINE MANSFIELD
QUOTED IN *BETWEEN TWO WORLDS* BY JOHN MIDDLETON MURRAY (1935)

Man has been worshipping cat for centuries and cat has every intention of keeping it that way.

—JOHN TICKNER
*TICKNER'S CATS* (1987)

This cat does more for the war effort than you do. He acts as a hot-water bottle and saves fuel and power.

—WINSTON CHURCHILL
QUOTED IN *THE COMPLETE LEXICAT*
BY MARK BRYANT (1992)

He looked on a woman as
an animal of domestic use, of
somewhat higher consideration
than a cat.

—HENRY FIELDING
*TOM JONES* (1749)

I will admit to feeling exceedingly proud when any cat has singled me out for notice; for, of course, every cat is really the most beautiful woman in the room. That is part of their deadly fascination.

—E. V. LUCAS (1868–1938)

It was then that he posed a question that as a cat hater I used to find easy to answer, but now as a cat lover I found most difficult. How do you summon up courage to dismiss a cat who is paying you the compliment of sitting on your lap?

—DEREK TANGYE
*A CAT IN THE WINDOW* (1962)

RIDDLES

Cats are a mysterious kind of folk. There is more passing in their minds than we are aware of.

—SIR WALTER SCOTT (1771–1832)

When I am playing with my cat, who knows whether she have more sport in dallying with me, than I have in gaming with her? We entertain one another with mutuall apish tricks. If I have my houre to begin or to refuse, so hath she hers.

—MICHEL DE MONTAIGNE
*APOLOGIE DE RAYMOND SEBOND*
TRANSLATED BY JOHN FLORIO
(1603)

Sometimes he will sit on the carpet
in front of you looking at you with eyes
so melting, so caressing and so human,
that they almost frighten you, for it
is impossible to believe that a soul is
not there.

—THEOPHILE GAUTIER (1811–1872)

Minnaloushe creeps through the grass

Alone, important and wise,

And lifts to the changing moon

His changing eyes.

—WILLIAM BUTLER YEATS
*THE CAT AND THE MOON* (1924)

As to its Eyes, Authors say that they shine in the Night, and see better at the full, and more dimly at the change of the Moon; as also that the Cat doth vary his Eyes with the Sun, the Apple of its Eye being long at Sun rise, round towards Noon, and not to be seen at all at night, but the whole Eye shining in the night. These appearances of the Cat's Eyes I am sure are true, but whether they answer to the times of the day, I never observed.

—WILLIAM SALMON
*THE COMPLEAT ENGLISH PHYSICIAN OR THE DRUGGIST'S SHOP OPENED (1693)*

I have often seen very intimate friendship between cat and dog, but I have never seen an intimate friendship between two cats.

—KAREL ČAPEK
***INTIMATE THINGS* (1935)**

The cat dwells within the circle of her own secret thoughts.

—AGNES REPPLIER
*THE FIRESIDE SPHINX* (1901)

If we take the case of cats, they say little, but they think a great deal; they conduct trains of reasoning.

—ANDREW LANG
**"AT THE SIGN OF THE SHIP"**
**IN *LONGMAN'S MAGAZINE***
**FEBRUARY 1905**

My cat neither laughs
nor cries; he is always
reasoning.

—MIGUEL DE UNAMUNO
*DEL SENTIMENTO TRAGICO
DE LA VIDA* (1912)

We cannot, without becoming cats, perfectly understand the cat mind.

—ST. GEORGE MIVART
*THE CAT* (1881)

But cats to me are strange, so strange

   I cannot sleep if one is near;

And though I'm sure I see those eyes,

   I'm not so sure a body's there!

      —W. H. DAVIES (1871–1940)

Who can tell what just criticisms Murr the cat may be passing on us beings of wider speculation?

—GEORGE ELIOT
*MIDDLEMARCH* (1871–1872)

He leaps and lightly
Walks upon sleep, his mind on the moon.
Nightly over the round world of men,
Over the roofs go his eyes and outcry.

—TED HUGHES
"ESTHER'S TOMCAT" IN *LUPERCAL*
(1960)

The cat with his phosphoric eyes, which serve him as lanterns, and sparks flying from his back, fearlessly haunts the darkness, where he encounters wandering phantoms, sorcerers, alchemists, necromancers, resurrectionists, lovers, pickpockets, assassins, drunken patrols, and all those obscene larvae which sally forth and do their work only at night. He has the air of having heard last Sunday's sermon, and readily rubs himself against the lame leg of Mephistopheles.

—THEOPHILE GAUTIER
**PREFACE TO *LES FLEURS DU MAL***
**BY CHARLES BAUDELAIRE (1868)**

I was awakened from a dream,

a dream entwined with cats,

by a cat's close presence.

In the darkness, by the bedside there

had loomed a form with shining hair—

squarish, immense-eyed, still.

Its whiskers pricked my lips:

I screamed.

    My daughter cried,

in just proportion terrified.

I realized that,

though only four, all skin and smiles,

my daughter is a lioness, taken as a cat.

—JOHN UPDIKE

"DAUGHTER" IN *COLLECTED POEMS*
*1953–1993* (1993)

The soul of another
is a mystery, and a
cat's soul even more so.

—ANTON CHEKHOV (1860–1904)

They call them stupid. They understand what we say better than we understand them. She understands all she wants to. Vindictive, too. Cruel. Her nature. Curious mice never squeal. Seem to like it. Wonder what I look like to her. Height of a tower? No, she can jump me.

—JAMES JOYCE

**LEOPOLD BLOOM RUMINATES ON HIS CAT IN** *ULYSSES* **(1922)**

I don't know how "smart" my cat is; I'm awfully afraid not very. Certainly I doubt that he ever thinks that he's thinking that I've just stepped on his tail. But I don't doubt at all that he finds having his tail stepped on painful, so when I do, I make it a point to apologize. Since being stepped on clearly pains my cat, I suppose it follows that he's conscious, at least from time to time.

—JERRY FODOR
*LONDON REVIEW OF BOOKS,*
*FEBRUARY 4, 1999*

No person has yet been able to pinpoint the purr conclusively.

—ELIZABETH MARSHALL THOMAS
*THE TRIBE OF THE TIGER* (1994)

A cat is an enigma but . . .
a very successful enigma.

—JEREMY ANGEL
*CATS' KINGDOM* (1985)

The things on a cat's mind must be wonderful beyond imagining.

—ROGER CARAS
*A CELEBRATION OF CATS* (1989)

An ample air, a warmer June,

Enfold me, and my wondering eye

Salutes a more imperial moon

Throned in a more resplendent sky

Than ever knew this pagan shore

Oh, strange! For you are with me too

And I who am a cat once more

Follow the woman that was you.

—LYTTON STRACHEY
"THE CAT" [1902] QUOTED
IN *LYTTON STRACHEY* BY
MICHAEL HOLROYD (REVISED
EDITION, 1969)

RANTS

CAT: A domestick animal that catches mice, commonly reckoned by naturalists the lowest order of the leonine species.

—SAMUEL JOHNSON
  *A DICTIONARY OF THE ENGLISH
  LANGUAGE* (1755)

Circe and Jezzie [two cats] did not enjoy the sea voyage, but they survived it, although there were moments when they seemed to be planning to throw themselves overboard, with the idea in mind, I am sure, of returning to earth later in the guise of spirochetes, or loose cellar steps, or United States Senators with voluminous, unevaluated rumors about my un-Siamese activities.

—JAMES THURBER
"MY SENEGALESE BIRDS AND SIAMESE CATS" IN *LANTERNS AND LANCES* (1961)

That vengeance I aske and crye,

By way of exclamation,

On all the whole nation

Of cattes wilde and tame;

God send them sorowe and shame!

That cat specially

That slew so cruelly

My little pretty sparrowe

That I brought up at Carowe.

    O cat of carlyshe kind,   [churlish]

The fiend was in thy mind

When thou my bird untwynde!   [destroyed]

I would thou haddest been blind!

The leopards savage,

The lions in their rage,

Might catch thee in their paws,

And gnaw thee in their jaws!

The serpents of Lybany

Might sting thee venemously!

The dragons with their tongues

Might poison thy liver and lungs!

The manticores of the mountains

Might feed them on thy brains!

—JOHN SKELTON
*"PHILLIP SPARROW"* (1568)

I have seen cats as stupid as any tax-payer.

—CARL VAN VECHTEN

***THE TIGER IN THE HOUSE*** (1921)

Apart from their obsession with hunting mice (and tinned cat food) cats are not exactly what a personnel manager would call ambitious.

—AKIF PIRINÇCI AND ROLF DEGEN
*CAT SENSE* (1994)

No living man, of low degree or high,

hates cats with such a deadly hate as I.

I hate their eyes, I hate the way they glare.

I see one and I'm gone, my hair

standing on end, nerves out of tune.

No cat will ever enter in my room.

—PIERRE RONSARD (1524–1585)

Cats are generally idiots when it comes to traffic. They just don't believe in it so therefore it is not there. They are no better than skunks in this regard.

—ROGER CARAS
*A CAT IS WATCHING* (1989)

A man has to work so hard so that something of his personality stays alive. A tomcat has it so easy, he has only to spray and his presence is there for years on rainy days.

—ALBERT EINSTEIN (1879–1955)

All that They do is venomous, and all that They think is evil, and when I take mine away (as I mean to do next week—in a basket), I shall first read in a book of statistics what is the wickedest part of London, and I shall leave It there, for I know of no one even among my neighbors quite as vile as to deserve such a gift.

—HILAIRE BELLOC
**"ON THEM" IN *ON NOTHING
AND KINDRED SUBJECTS* (1908)**

Do not throw rocks at cats. It merely frightens the poor creatures, and you never hit them.

—HENRY MITCHELL
*THE ESSENTIAL EARTHMAN* (1981)

Cat: A soft indestructible automaton provided by nature to be kicked when things go wrong in the domestic circle.

—AMBROSE BIERCE
*A CYNIC'S WORD BOOK*
*(THE DEVIL'S DICTIONARY)* (1906)

Squalid Things:
The inside of a cat's ear.

—SEI SHŌNAGON

*THE PILLOW BOOK* [10TH CENTURY]
TRANSLATED BY IVAN MORRIS
(1967)

The cat is a very false and faithless and thievish animal which neither by caresses and good feeling nor by blows and imprisonment can be so tamed that it will not scratch and steal. It is and remains always a malignant deceiver.

—*NATURAL HISTORY FOR CHILDREN*
(1809)
QUOTED IN *A CELEBRATION OF CATS* BY ROGER CARAS (1989)

The cat is an unfaithful domestic
animal, only kept through necessity
to suppress another domestic animal
that incommodes us still more.

—GEORGES-LOUIS LECLERC, COMTE
DE BUFFON
*HISTOIRE NATURELLE, GÉNÉRALE
ET PARTICULIÈRE* (1749–1788)

One must acknowledge that the cat does nothing to modify the opinion in which it is held. It is entirely unpopular, but cares as little about this as it does about the Grand Turk.

—ALEXANDRE DUMAS
*HISTOIRE DE MES BÊTES*
(1892 EDITION)

The trouble with a kitten is

THAT

Eventually it becomes a

CAT.

—OGDEN NASH

"THE KITTEN" *THE FACE IS FAMILIAR*
(1940)

"You know, Trotwood,
I don't want to swing
a cat. I never do swing
a cat."

—CHARLES DICKENS
*DAVID COPPERFIELD* (1849-1850)

I love Wagner, but the music I prefer is that of a cat hung by its tail outside of a window, trying to stick to the panes of glass with its claws. There is an odd grating on the glass which I find at the same time strange, irritating, and singularly harmonious.

—CHARLES BAUDELAIRE

**QUOTED IN *THE TIGER IN THE HOUSE* BY CARL VAN VECHTEN (1921)**

I might describe the utility of the ichneumon, the crocodile, and the cat, but I have no wish to be tedious.

—CICERO
*DE DEORUM NATURA*
(1ST CENTURY A.D.)

The conceit that a cat has nine lives has cost at least nine lives in ten of the whole race of 'em.

—ALEXANDER POPE (1688–1744)

[Their] disingenuity of character is betrayed by the obliquity of their movements and the ambiguity of their looks.

—"CAT" IN *ENCYCLOPEDIA BRITANNICA* (THIRD EDITION 1787)

It is assumed that I love cats. It makes as much sense to say that I love cats as to say that a heroin addict loves heroin.

—GERMAINE GREER
**"CONFESSIONS OF A CAT ADDICT"**
**IN *THE OLDIE* MARCH 3, 1993**

Now I am not a cat man, but a dog man, and all felines can tell this at a glance—a sharp, vindictive glance.

—JAMES THURBER

"MY SENEGALESE BIRDS AND SIAMESE CATS" IN *LANTERNS AND LANCES* (1961)

[Cats] follow the self-interest principle with all the natural tyranny of a spoilt child.

—AKIF PIRINÇCI AND ROLF DEGEN
*CAT SENSE* (1994)

Cats are no answer to anybody's bird problem, because then you would have cats.

—HENRY MITCHELL
*THE ESSENTIAL EARTHMAN* (1981)

A screech-owl is worth a dozen cats and not one cat in twenty will tackle a rat.

—*THE OOLOGIST MAGAZINE* (c. 1915)

Why cats were given
such terrific peripheral
vision when they spend
so much time looking
down their noses is
difficult to understand.

—ROGER CARAS
*A CAT IS WATCHING* (1989)

Most of the poets who have written verse about cats would have been better employed composing advertisements for detergents.

—BEVERLEY NICHOLS (1899–1983)

There is no way of writing about cats that allows you to be thought of as a sane and sensible person.

—BRUCE FOGLE
*THE CAT'S MIND* (1991)

Cat: A deceitful animal and when enraged extremely spiteful.

—NOAH WEBSTER

*AN AMERICAN DICTIONARY OF THE ENGLISH LANGUAGE* (1828)

You know what a flattering, snuggling but also false, spiteful, faithless animal the housecat is. How it scratches and bites and robs and steals! There is no worse thief than a cat . . . For that reason many people cannot endure it, and some find cats so repellent to their natures that they fall in a faint if a cat so much as comes close to them.

—LUDWIG JERRER

*NATURAL HISTORY FOR THE YOUNG* (1835) QUOTED IN *A CELEBRATION OF CATS* BY ROGER CARAS (1989)

I have never had so expensive a Christmas present and by expensive . . . I mean what it has cost me. When I go away, I store the silver in the bank for fifty cents a month and I store her in posh cat-houses for a dollar a day . . . my cleaning bills and those of my friends (the few I have left) are staggering. She would rather starve than eat anything so non-U as Puss 'n Boots . . . Her hospital bills have run into four figures and mine, after getting the bills, have not been inconsiderable—when I am not insomniac, I am in a dead faint.

—JEAN STAFFORD
"GEORGE ELIOT: A MEDICAL STUDY"
(1957) IN *KNOWING CATS* EDITED BY
ALAN HARVEY (1977)

Another time, when my parents were away, I am ashamed to say that the footsteps and whispering in the garden under my window grew so alarming that I actually telephoned to the Police. Who came and said it was Cats. Cats! It would be cats; they knew I didn't like them, the devils.

—GWEN RAVERAT
*PERIOD PIECE: A CAMBRIDGE CHILDHOOD* (1952)

Cats are not overly bright. The reason a house cat cannot be trained to do many things is not only its "independence," it just isn't as smart as a dog.

—EDWARD HOAGLAND
**"TIGER BRIGHT" IN** *HEART'S DESIRE*
**(1988)**

Cats are ungrateful. "Feed a dog for three days," says a Japanese proverb, "and he will remember your kindness for three years; feed a cat for three years and she will forget your kindness in three days." Cats are mischievious: they tear the mattings, and make holes in the shō̄ji, and sharpen their claws upon the pillars of tokonoma. Cats are under a curse: only the cat and the venomous serpent wept not at the death of Buddha; and these shall never enter into the bliss of the Gokuraku. For all these reasons, and others too numerous to relate, cats are not much loved in Izumo, and are compelled to pass the greater part of their lives out of doors.

—LAFCADIO HEARN
"IN A JAPANESE GARDEN" IN
*GLIMPSES OF UNFAMILIAR JAPAN*
(1894)

Confound the cats! All cats—alway—
Cats of all colours, black, white, grey;
By night a nuisance and by day—
    Confound the cats!

—ORLANDO DOBBIN (1807–1890)
    "A DITHYRAMB ON CATS"

Ware the cat, Parot,
ware the fals cat!

—JOHN SKELTON
**"SPEKE, PAROT" (1568)**

A tortoise-shell cat having a fit
in a platter of tomatoes.

—MARK TWAIN
DESCRIPTION OF J. M. W. TURNER'S
PAINTING *THE SLAVE SHIP*

People with insufficient personalities are fond of cats. These people adore being ignored.

—HENRY MORGAN

**QUOTED IN WILLIAM COLE**
*THE CAT-HATER'S HANDBOOK*
**(1963)**

CUISINE

And the briske Mouse may feast her selfe with

 crums

Till that the green-ey'd Kitling comes.

—ROBERT HERRICK
"A COUNTRY LIFE" IN *COMPLETE
POETRY* EDITED BY J. MAX PATRICK
(1963)

The beggar's dog and
the widow's cat
Feed them and thou
wilt grow fat.

—WILLIAM BLAKE
*AUGURIES OF INNOCENCE*
**[1801–1803] (1863)**

Mr. Leonard, a very intelligent friend of mine, saw a cat catch a trout, by darting upon it in deep clear water, at the mill at Weaford, near Lichfield. The cat belonged to Mr. Stanley, who had often seen her catch fish in the same manner in the summer when the mill-pool was drawn so low that the fish could be seen. I have heard of other cats taking fish in shallow water as they stood on the bank. This seems to be a natural art of taking their prey in cats, which their acquired delicacy by domestication has in general prevented them from using, though their desire of eating fish continues in its original strength.

—ERASMUS DARWIN
*ZOONOMIA* (1794-1796)

Three, down, through windows
Dawn leaping cats, all barred brown, grey
Whiskers aflame
   bits of mouse on the tongue.

—GARY SNYDER
"A BERRY FEAST" IN
*THE BACK COUNTRY* (1968)

A cat is something between a rabbit and a squirrel with a flavour of its own. It is delicious. Don't drown your kittens, eat 'em.

—HENRY LABOUCHERE
**QUOTED IN *CONSUMING PASSIONS*
BY JONATHON GREEN (1985)**

"I stayed in the same house with a pieman once, sir, and a wery nice man he was—reg'lar clever chap, too—make pies out o' anything, he could. . . . 'Mr. Weller,' says he, a-squeezing my hand wery hard, and vispering in my ear—'don't mention this here agin—but it's the seasonin' as does it. They're all made of them noble animals,' says he, a-pointin' to a wery nice little tabby kitten, 'and I seasons 'em for beef-steak, weal, or kidney, 'cording to demand. And more than that,' says he, 'I can make a weal a beef-steak, or a beef-steak a kidney, or any one on 'em a mutton, at a minute's notice, just as the market changes, and appetites wary.'"

"He must have been a very ingenious young man, that, Sam," said Mr. Pickwick, with a slight shudder.

—CHARLES DICKENS
*THE PICKWICK PAPERS* (1836)

The cat laps the moonbeams in a bowl
of water
Thinking them to be milk.

—*POEMS FROM THE SANSKRIT*
**TRANSLATED BY JOHN BROUGH**
**(1968)**

Lat take a cat and fostre hym wel with milk

And tendre flessh, and make his couche of silk,

And lat hym seen a mous go by the wal,

Anon he weyveth[1] milk and flessh and al,

And every deyntee that is in that hous,

Swich appetit he hath to ete a mous.

Lo, heere hath lust his dominacioun,

And appetit fleemeth[2] discrecioun.

—GEOFFREY CHAUCER
"THE MANCIPLE'S TALE" IN *THE CANTERBURY TALES* (1380–1400)

[1] ignores
[2] chases away

Only—the thought disturbs him—
He's noticed once or twice,
The times are somehow breeding
A nimbler race of mice.

—SIR ALEXANDER GRAY (1882–1968)
"ON A CAT, AGEING"

The lapping of milk out of a saucer is what one's human thirst cannot sympathise with. It seems as if there could be no satisfaction in such a series of atoms of drink.

—LEIGH HUNT

**"THE CAT BY THE FIRE"** IN *THE SEER, OR, COMMON-PLACES REFRESHED* (1840)

It was only the round of Nature. The worms eat a noxious something in the ground. The birds eat the worms. Calvin eats the birds. We eat—no, we do not eat Calvin. There the chain stops. When you ascend the scale of being, and come to an animal that is, like ourselves, inedible, you have arrived at a result where you can rest. Let us respect the cat. He completes an edible chain.

—CHARLES DUDLEY WARNER
*MY SUMMER IN A GARDEN* (1870)

A cat

I keep that plays about my house

Grown fat

With eating many a miching mouse.

—ROBERT HERRICK

**"HIS GRANGE, OR PRIVATE
WEALTH" IN** *COMPLETE POETRY*
**EDITED BY J. MAX PATRICK (1963)**

There is a propensity belonging
to common house-cats that is very
remarkable; I mean their violent fond-
ness for fish, which appears to be their
most favorite food: and yet nature in
this instance seems to have planted in
them an appetite that, unassisted, they
know not how to gratify: for of all the
quadrupeds cats are the least disposed
towards water; and will not, when they
can avoid it, deign to wet a foot,
much less plunge into that element.

—GILBERT WHITE
*THE NATURAL HISTORY OF
SELBOURNE* (1788)

But the Kittencats who snatch

　　Rudely for their food, or scratch,

Grow to Tomcats gaunt and gory,—

　　Theirs is quite another story.

Cats like these are put away

　　By the dread S.P.C.A.

Or to trusting Aunts and Sisters

　　Sold as sable Muffs and Wristers.

—OLIVER HERFORD
*THE KITTEN'S GARDEN OF VERSES*
(1911)

A gentleman had a favorite cat whom he taught to sit at the dinner-table where it behaved very well. He was in the habit of putting any scraps he left on to the cat's plate. One day puss did not take his place punctually, but presently appeared with two mice, one of which he placed on his master's plate, the other on its own.

—BEATRIX POTTER

*THE JOURNAL OF BEATRIX POTTER FROM 1881 TO 1897 (1966)*

When food mysteriously goes
The chances are that Pussy knows
More than she leads you to suppose.

And hence there is no need for you,
If Puss declines a meal or two,
To feel her pulse or make ado.

—ANON

The place was a paradise of cats. "Are all these your own cats?" "Oh, dear, no, some of them are, and some are cats who regularly come to have tea, and some are still other cats, not invited by us, but who seem to find out about this time of day that tea will be going."

—THOMAS HARDY
**QUOTED IN *THOMAS HARDY***
**BY EDMUND BLUNDEN (1967)**

A correspondent assures me that a cat in his house used to put her paws into jugs of milk having too narrow a mouth for her head. A kitten of this cat soon learned the same trick, and practised it ever afterwards, whenever there was an opportunity.

—CHARLES DARWIN
*THE DESCENT OF MAN* (1871)

Cats are cut out for the
sybaritic life.

—AKIF PIRINÇCI AND ROLF DEGEN
*CAT SENSE* (1994)

There are more ways of killing
a cat than of choking her with
cream.

—CHARLES KINGSLEY (1819–1875)

The cat will eat an insect now and then, I don't know why, nor do I know why, having eaten some few, he doesn't go on to take them regularly. We have analogous yens and preferences, most people; pickles, liver, rhubarb, etc. Claggart may believe they tone up the system.

—WILLIAM SERVICE
*OWL* (1969)

They'll take suggestion
as a cat laps milk.

—WILLIAM SHAKESPEARE
***THE TEMPEST*** (1623)

I have made a practice, from their earliest kittenhood, of training them to place no reliance or affection upon anybody but themselves. In vain. Chatsworth is an arrant coward, and Chatterly practically an idiot . . . they sleep all day in the sitting-room, in the intervals of mewing at me for more food. The mew of a Siamese cat is the most piercing thing I know, and they eat about two pounds each of raw meat every day. Worm powders increase their appetite.

—T. H. WHITE

*ENGLAND HAVE MY BONES* (1936)

OBSERVATIONS

Cats are to be loved because
they are cats, and for no other
reason.

—*THE SPECTATOR,*
26 FEBRUARY 1898

If a cat spoke, it would say things like, "Hey, I don't see the problem here."

—ROY BLOUNT, JR. (1941– )

Every dog has his day
and a cat two Sundays.

—PROVERB

A cat may look at a king
And sure I may look at an ugly thing.

—ANON

The Kitty-Cat Bird, he moped and he cried

Then a real Cat came with a Mouth so Wide,

That the Kitty-Cat Bird just hopped inside;

"At last I'm myself!"—and he up and died.

Did the Kitty—the Kitty-Cat Bird.

—THEODORE ROETHKE
"THE KITTY-CAT BIRD" IN
COLLECTED POEMS (1966)

There was a young person of Smyrna,
Whose Grandmother threatened to
burn her;
    But she seized on the cat
    And said, "Granny, burn that!
You incongruous old woman of
Smyrna."

—EDWARD LEAR
*THE OXFORD BOOK OF LIGHT
VERSE* EDITED BY W. H. AUDEN
(1938)

The Owl looked up to the stars above
    And sang to a small guitar,
"O lovely Pussy! O Pussy, my love,
What a beautiful Pussy you are,
    You are,
    You are!
What a beautiful Pussy you are!"

—EDWARD LEAR
**"THE OWL AND THE PUSSY CAT" IN
THE *OXFORD BOOK OF LIGHT
VERSE* EDITED BY W. H. AUDEN
(1938)**

Cats have nine lives, onions and women seven skins.

—PROVERB

The Dog gives himself
the Airs of a Cat.

—RICHARD STEELE (1672–1729)

A cat once bitten by a snake
fears even rope.

—ARAB PROVERB

There wanst was two cats in Kilkenny,
Aitch thought there was one cat too many;
    So they quarrelled and fit,
    They scratched and they bit,
    Till, excepting the nails
    And the tips of their tails,
Instead of two cats, there wasn't any.

—IRISH FOLK VERSE

All cats are grey in the dark.

—THOMAS LODGE
*A MARGARITE OF AMERICA* (1596)

Cats of good breed hunt
better fat than lean.

—BENVENUTO CELLINI (1500–1571)

There once was a Grand Duke of Baden

Said "The Things that go on in My Garden!

    I really can't stand;

    Not a Cat in the Land

But gives itself Heirs in my Garden."

—H. H. MUNRO ("SAKI")
*THE SQUARE EGG* (1929)

Cat mighty dignified till de dog come by.

—PROVERB

Send not a cat for lard.

—GEORGE HERBERT
***OUTLANDISH PROVERBS* (1640)**

The cat does play,
And after slay.

—*THE NEW ENGLAND PRIMER* (c. 1688)

Care killed a cat.

—PROVERB

A scalded cat dreads even cold water.

—PROVERB

A bad cat deserves a bad rat.

—PROVERB

He that laugheth not at all hath the nature of an old cat.

—THOMAS FULLER
*GNOMOLOGIA* (1732)

Enough to make a cat laugh.

—SAYING

Cats, like men, are flatterers.

—WALTER SAVAGE LANDOR
**"LA FONTAINE AND DE LA
ROCHEFOUCAULD" IN *IMAGINARY
CONVERSATIONS OF LITERARY MEN
AND STATESMEN* (1824–1854)**

Cats that go ratting don't wear gloves.

—HENRY ADAMS
*DEMOCRACY* (1880)

When the cat's away,
the mice dance.

—JEAN-ANTOINE DE BAÏF
*MIMES, ENSEIGNMENTS ET
PROVERBES* (1576)

Cats and children are alike in the way they never quite give up the bad habits they acquire when young.

—ABBÉ DE SAINT-CYRAN (1581–1643)
*LETTRES À SA NIECE*

The cat invites the mouse to a feast.

—THOMAS FULLER
***GNOMOLOGIA*** (1732)

It is not worth while going around the world to count the cats in Zanzibar.

—HENRY DAVID THOREAU
*WALDEN* (1854)

Cats may have had their goose

Cooked by tobacco-juice;

Still why deny its use

Thoughtfully taken?

—C. S. CALVERLEY

"ODE TO TOBACCO" (1862)

Do cats eat bats?—Do bats eat cats?

—LEWIS CARROLL
***ALICE IN WONDERLAND* (1865)**

[The Cheshire Cat] vanished quite slowly, beginning with the end of its tail, and ending with the grin, which remained some time after the rest of it had gone.

—LEWIS CARROLL
***ALICE IN WONDERLAND*** (1865)

Cats and monkeys, monkeys and cats—
all human life is there.

—HENRY JAMES
*THE MADONNA OF THE FUTURE*
(1879)

A harmless necessary cat.

**—WILLIAM SHAKESPEARE**
*THE MERCHANT OF VENICE* (1600)

"Cats are not dogs!" There is only one place where you can hear good things like that thrown off quite casually in the general run of conversation, and that is the bar parlour of the Angler's Rest.

—P. G. WODEHOUSE
**"THE STORY OF WEBSTER" IN**
*MULLINER NIGHTS* **(1933)**

Cats are intended
to teach us that not
everything in nature
has a function.

—GARRISON KEILLOR (1942– )

It's almost as if we're put here on earth to show how silly they aren't.

—RUSSELL HOBAN (1925- )

Wherever a cat sits, there shall happiness be found.

—STANLEY SPENCER (1891–1959)

God save all here,
except the cat.

—IRISH GREETING

The differences between languages are interesting. Cat: purr-purr (English), ron-ron (French), schnurr-schnurr (German).

—MURRAY SCHAFER
*THE TUNING OF THE WORLD* (1977)

A cat with a straw tail shouldn't sit with her back to the fire.

—PROVERB

Nature in her wisdom has evolved her cats to be somewhat insensitive to hot and cold, but why has she made them indifferent to the smell of their own hind ends when they are about to go up in flames?

—ROGER CARAS
*A CAT IS WATCHING* (1989)

A dog is prose; a cat is a poem.

—JEAN BURDEN (1914- )

When cat and mouse
agree, the farmer has
no chance.

—PROVERB

It doesn't matter if a cat is black or white, as long as it catches mice.

—DENG XIAOPING (1904–1997)

Only astrophysicists knew about the Internet 20 years ago. Today my cat has a Web site.

—PRESIDENT BILL CLINTON
QUOTED BY RICK VAN SANT,
SCRIPPS HOWARD NEWS SERVICE,
FEBRUARY 10, 1997

One cat in a house is a sign
of loneliness, two of barrenness,
and three of sodomy.

—EDWARD DAHLBERG
"MOBY DICK: A HAMITIC DREAM"
IN *ALMS FOR OBLIVION* (1964)

No matter how much cats fight, there
always seem to be plenty of kittens.

—ABRAHAM LINCOLN (1809–1865)

Alfred de Musset
Called his cat Pusset.
His accent was affected.
That was only to be expected.

—M. E. HARE (1886–1967)

Old cats mean young mice.

—ITALIAN SAYING

There are three animals whose tails, eyes and lives are of the same worth: a calf; a filly for common work; a cat; excepting the cat that shall watch the king's barn.

—HYWEL DDA, PRINCE OF SOUTH
WALES CODES ENACTED c. 940

# CELEBRATING
# CATS

Cat: one hell of nice animal, often mistaken for a meatloaf.

—B. KLIBAN
*CAT* (1975)

Mrs. Tatters uneasy that we did not come down stairs at the usual hour Scratched at our Door for admittance, came on the bed to me and lay there till Ten o'clock at night Purring all the Time—a day of Tenderness and Sensibility.

—ELEANOR BUTLER
JOURNAL DECEMBER 2, 1785.
QUOTED IN *A YEAR WITH THE LADIES OF LLANGOLLEN* EDITED BY ELIZABETH MAVOR (1984)

Graceful Things: One day by the balustrade before a set of thin head-blinds I saw a pretty cat with a red collar and a white name tag. He looked very elegant as he walked along, pulling his anchor cord and biting it.

—SEI SHNŌAGON
*THE PILLOW BOOK* [10TH CENTURY]
TRANSLATED BY IVAN MORRIS
(1967)

They had a cat named 208 . . . My friend said that 208 thought he was the only cat left in the world, not having seen another cat since he was a tiny kitten . . . When you played with that cat, he really bit you. Stroke 208's fur and he'd try to disembowel your hand as if it were a belly stuffed with extra-soft intestines.

—RICHARD BRAUTIGAN
"ROOM 208, HOTEL TROUT FISHING IN AMERICA" *TROUT FISHING IN AMERICA* (1967)

Praise be to thee, O Ra, exalted Sekhem, thou art the Great Cat, the avenger of the gods, and the judge of words, and the president of the sovereign chiefs and the governor of the holy Circle; thou art indeed the bodies of the Great Cat.

—FROM "THE SEVENTY-FIVE PRAISES OF RA," AN INSCRIPTION ON THE WALL OF A ROYAL EGYPTIAN TOMB IN THEBES, QUOTED IN *THE EVERLASTING CAT* BY MILDRED KIRK (1977)

One cat just leads to another.

—ERNEST HEMINGWAY (1899–1961)

For I will consider my cat Jeoffrey.

For he is the servant of the Living God and
daily serving him.

For at the first glance of the glory of God in
the East he worships in his way.

For this is done by wreathing his body seven
times round with elegant quickness.

For then he leaps up to catch the musk, which
is the blessing of God upon his prayer.

For he rolls upon prank to work it in.

For having done duty and received blessing
he begins to consider himself.

For this he performs in ten degrees.

For first he looks upon his fore-paws to see if
they are clean.

For secondly he kicks up behind to clear away
there.

For thirdly he works it upon stretch with the
fore-paws extended.

For fourthly he sharpens his claws by wood.

For fifthly he washes himself.

For sixthly he rolls upon wash.

For seventhly he fleas himself, that he may
not be interrupted upon the beat.

For eighthly he rubs himself against a post.

For ninthly he looks up for his instructions.

For tenthly he goes in quest of food.

. . . . . . . . .

For there is nothing sweeter than his peace
when at rest.

For there is nothing brisker than his life when in
motion.

—CHRISTOPHER SMART
*JUBILATE AGNO* (1758–1763)

I frequently suffered a good deal from the presence of the same Hodge. I recollect him one day scrambling up Dr. Johnson's breast, apparently with much satisfaction, while my friend, smiling and half-whistling, rubbed down his back, and pulled him by the tail; and when I observed he was a fine cat, saying "Why, yes, Sir, but I have had cats whom I liked better than this"; and then, as if perceiving Hodge to be out of countenance, adding "but he is a very fine cat, a very fine cat indeed."

—JAMES BOSWELL
*THE LIFE OF SAMUEL JOHNSON*
**(1791)**

Each individual cat differs in
as many ways as possible from
each other individual cat.

—CARL VAN VECHTEN
*THE TIGER IN THE HOUSE* (1921)

His nose touches his back, touches his hind

  paws too,

Every patch of fur is raked, and scraped, and

  smoothed;

What more has Goethe done, what more could

  Voltaire do?

> —HIPPOLYTE TAINE
>
> *DOUZES SONNETS INÉDITS DE*
> *TAINE* (1893)

Familiar spirit, genius, judge,
the cat presides—inspires
events that he appears to spurn,
half goblin and half god!

—CHARLES BAUDELAIRE
"CATS" IN *LES FLEURS DU MAL*
(1857) TRANSLATED BY RICHARD
HOWARD (1982)

. . . Musical instruments took their first rise from the notes of birds, and other melodious animals; and what, says he, was more natural than for the first ages of mankind to imitate the voice of a cat that lived under the same roof with them? He added that the cat had contributed more to harmony than any other animal; as we are not only beholden to her for this wind instrument [the cat-call], but for our string music in general.

—JOSEPH ADDISON
"DISSERTATION ON THE CAT-CALL"
IN *SPECTATOR NO. 361* (1712)

What marvelous vitality a kitten has. It is really something very beautiful the way life bubbles over in the little creatures. They rush about, and mew, and spring; dance on their hind legs, embrace everything with their front ones, roll over and over, lie on their backs and kick. They don't know what to do with themselves, they are so full of life.

—JEROME K. JEROME
*IDLE THOUGHTS OF AN IDLE FELLOW* (1886)

Hell would have made
the cat its courier could
it have controverted
feline pride!

—CHARLES BAUDELAIRE
**"CATS" IN *LES FLEURS DU MAL***
**(1857) TRANSLATED BY RICHARD**
**HOWARD (1982)**

—Cruel, but composed and bland,

Dumb, inscrutable and grand,

So Tiberius might have sat

Had Tiberius been a cat.

—MATTHEW ARNOLD

"MATTHIAS" IN *POEMS* EDITED BY

KATHERINE ALLOTT (1965)

The animals which merit particular attention are cats, dogs, and fast horses. The cat is less reputable than the other two just named, because she is less wasteful; she may even serve a useful purpose.

—THORSTEIN VEBLEN
*THE THEORY OF THE LEISURE CLASS* (1899)

A kitten is in the animal world what a rosebud is in a garden.

—ROBERT SOUTHEY (1774–1843)

The Cat and the Archbishop, sitting together as they generally did, make a picture in themselves—the former looking, according to my recollections, the more austere theologian of the two.

—SIR HENRY HOLLAND
ON THE ARCHBISHOP OF TARANTO
AND HIS CAT DESDEMONA IN
*RECOLLECTIONS OF PAST LIFE*
(1872)

He had a special vocabulary for defining the various grades of feline excellence, beginning with "pussum" and culminating in MOG—the supreme cat, the Platonic cat, the cat in the mind of God, the Great One of the Night Time.

—CECIL GRAY
***PETER WARLOCK*** (1934)

She moved through the garden in glory, because

She had very long claws at the end of her paws.

Her back was arched, her tail was high,

A green fire glared in her vivid eye;

And all the Toms, though never so bold,

Quailed at the martial Marigold.

> —RICHARD GARNETT
> "MARIGOLD" IN *THE CATS'*
> *NEWSPAPER* (c. 1880)

I salute in you, calm thinker, two exquisite virtues: skepticism and sweetness.

—FRANÇOIS ELIE JULES LEMAÎTRE
(1853–1914)

The cat is unfairly calumniated. Man will not pardon his pride; a cat feels that it is beneath him to be forced to win the affection of a superior being who knows his price and will not give his friendship unreservedly. Nothing is more pleasant to caress or more faithful than a cat, to one who deserves him; but he will not put up with bad treatment and he can be jealous and touchy in the extreme.

—CAMILLE SAINT-SAËNS
*AU COURANT DE LA VIE* (1914)

I have (and long shall have) a great white nimble
   cat

A king upon a mouse, a strong foe to the rat,

Fine eares, long taile he hath, with Lions curbed
   clawe,

Which oft he lifteth up, and stayes his lifted pawe,

Deepe musing to himselfe, which after-mewing
   showes,

Till with lickt beard, his eye of fire espie his foes.

—SIR PHILIP SIDNEY
*ARCADIA* (1593)

Cats . . . have succeeded one another through the Tertiary epoch, therefore, for thousands, or more probably, millions, of years . . . [and], in their capacity of butchering machines, have undergone a steady though slow and gradual improvement.

—T. H. HUXLEY
*NATURAL RIGHTS AND POLITICAL RIGHTS* (1890)

Of all God's creatures there is only one that cannot be made the slave of the lash. That one is the cat. If man could be crossed with the cat it would improve man, but it would deteriorate the cat.

—MARK TWAIN
***NOTEBOOK*** (1935)

What woman has this old cat's graces?

—SIR FRANCIS MEYNELL (1891–1975)
*MAN AND BEAST*

No more complete example of a perfectly organized being can well be found than that supplied by a member of what has no inconsiderable claim to be regarded as the highest mammalian family—the family Felidae.

—ST. GEORGE MIVART
*THE CAT* (1881)

A cat pours his body on the floor like water. It is restful just to see him.

—WILLIAM LYON PHELPS (1865-1943)

Cats are the only animals which are really owned by clubs and corps and companies. Those artificial persons seldom, if ever, own dogs. . . . A dog must have a master . . . A cat, being in reality its own master, does excellently under a corporate body. Some of the lordliest and most self-satisfied cats we have ever met were club cats and college cats.

—*THE SPECTATOR*
26 FEBRUARY 1898

I speak for cats.

—EMILE ZOLA (1840–1902)
**"LE PARADIS DES CHATS"**

Men ride many miles
Cats tread many tiles
Both hazard their necks in the fray;
Only Cats, when they fall
From a house or a wall,
Keep their feet, mount their tails,
and away!

—THOMAS FLATMAN
"AN APPEAL TO CATS IN THE
BUSINESS OF LOVE" IN
*POEMS AND SONGS* (1674)

For years I matched cats in friends' houses, cats in shops, cats on farms, cats in the street, cats on walls, cats in memory, with that gentle blue-grey purring creature which for me was the cat, the Cat, never to be replaced.

—DORIS LESSING
*PARTICULARLY CATS* (1967)

Take, Lord, this soul of furred unblemished

    worth,

The sum of all I loved and caught on earth.

Quick was my holy purpose and my cause.

I die into the mercy of thy claws.

> —ANNE STEVENSON
> "EPITAPH FOR A GOOD MOUSER" IN
> *SELECTED POEMS 1956–1986* (1987)

Oh what can be happening pray what are they at?

Oh why am I slowly turning into a cat?

Is it Zeus is responsible, tired of my love

Does he send me outside with the puss cats

    to rove?

Or indifferent rather, quite sick of it all,

Is he simply letting Hera have her way with

    a rival?

Oh look at my beautiful coat and my handsome

    whiskers,

I shall be most loved of all the young cats and I

    shall be called Friskers.

—STEVIE SMITH
"FRISKERS, OR GODS AND MEN"
IN *THE COLLECTED POEMS OF
STEVIE SMITH* (1975)

The cat is thus playing a double game: at the center it has the vision of a beast of prey, on both side the vision of the victim. The lion and the gazelle are both present in its eye.

—JEAN-LOUIS HUE
*KÄTZEN: EINE LIEBESERKLÄRUNG*
**(1984)**

Cats never stop
investigating the
world once they
learn it is there.

—ROGER CARAS
*A CAT IS WATCHING* (1989)

A cat is better than you are, more honest, more graceful, smarter for her size, better coordinated and infinitely more beautiful.

—LEONORE FLEISCHER
*THE CAT'S PYJAMAS* (1982)

Bathsheba: to whom none has ever
  said scat
No worthier cat
Ever sat on a mat
Or caught a rat
Requies-cat.

—JOHN GREENLEAF WHITTIER
(1807–1892)
**"FOR A LITTLE GIRL MOURNING HER
FAVORITE CAT"**

If truth be told, and however impossible the idea, I would like to have known every cat that has ever lived.

—ROGER CARAS

*A CELEBRATION OF CATS* (1989)

There is nothing transitory about a cat, aside

from the

individual knack of survival;

it is the most ancient of our

animals. A dead cat never

has the look of finality that

a dead dog does.

—ELEANOR CLARK
*ROME AND A VILLA* (1952)

A cat does not want to die with the smell of humanity in his nostrils and the noise of humanity in his delicate peaked ears.

—ALAN DEVOE
*PHUDD HILL* (1937)

There is not a single case on record of a cat who died in his bed.

—FRANÇOIS COPPÉE (1842–1908)

If we feel sorry for the dying
cat that cannot understand what is
happening to it, we should remember
that it has one enormous advantage
over us: it has no fear of death, which
is something we humans must carry
with us throughout our long lives.

—DESMOND MORRIS
*CATLORE* (1987)

A cat has absolute emotional honesty.

—ERNEST HEMINGWAY (1899–1961)

You can spoil a child and it can become a nuisance. You can spoil a dog and everyone except its owner is certain to suffer. A cat on the other hand, however luscious may be the bribes, remains cool and collected. . . . Indulgence never goes to its head. It observes flattery instead of accepting it.

—DEREK TANGYE
*A CAT IN THE WINDOW* (1962)

Most all fighting creatures sport either whiskers or beards; it seems a law of Dame Nature. Witness the boar, the tiger, the cougar, man, the leopard, the ram, the cat—all warriors, and all whiskerandoes.

—HERMAN MELVILLE
*WHITE JACKET* (1850)

Its tail was a plume of such magnificence that it almost wore the cat.

—HUGH LEONARD
***ROVER AND OTHER CATS* (1992)**

I saw the most beautiful cat today. It was sitting by the side of the road, its two front feet neatly and graciously together. Then it gravely swished around its tail to completely and snugly encircle itself. It was so fit and beautfully neat, that gesture, and so self-satisfied—so complacent.

—ANNE MORROW LINDBERGH
*BRING ME A UNICORN* (1972)

WHO'S WHO

**Adams, Henry** (1838–1918) Historian, novelist, grandson, and great-grandson of presidents of the United States.

**Addison, Joseph** (1672–1719) English essayist, poet, and statesman.

**Angel, Jeremy** English biologist and photographer who helped set up a cat-study center in Japan and wrote a book about it.

**Anon** Prolific author.

**Arnold, Matthew** (1822–1888) English poet and author, the leading critic of his day.

**Bardot, Brigitte** (1934– ) Famous animal lover.

**Barron, Oswald** (1868–1939) Author and antiquary, essayist in the *London Evening News*.

**Baudelaire, Charles** (1821–1867) Generally unhappy French poet.

**Beachcroft, T. O.** (1902–1988) English short story writer.

**Beerbohm, Max** (1872–1926) Clever, delicate, extremely witty British caricaturist and essayist.

**Belloc, Hilaire** (1870–1953) Often savage poet and satirist.

**Bierce, Ambrose** (1842?–1914) American short story writer and journalist.

**Bishop, Elizabeth** (1911–1979) American poet whose reputation has been rising constantly since her death.

**Blake, William** (1757–1827) English mystic and poet.

**Blount, Roy Jr.** (1941– ) American humorist.

**Bombeck, Erma** (1927–1996) Hymnist of American domestic humor.

**Boothroyd, Basil** (1910–1988) English journalist and broadcaster, author of numerous pleasant lightweight books.

**Boswell, James** (1740–1795) Scot whose biography of Samuel Johnson may be the best of its kind ever written.

**Brautigan, Richard** (1935–1984) Once wildly popular American short story writer and novelist.

**Brough, John** (1917–1984) Translator.

**Bryant, Mark** (1953– ) English author of a book mostly about cat names.

**Buffon, George-Louis Leclerc, comte de** (1707–1788) French naturalist, author of the enormous *Histoire Naturelle* (in 36 volumes, plus eight more added by lesser folk after his death).

**Burden, Jean** (1914– ) American poet, author, editor, pet expert.

**Butler, Eleanor** (1739?–1829) One of the two famous Ladies of Llangollen, Irishwomen who eloped to live together in North Wales, where they were visited by many of the most prominent figures of their time.

**Butler, Samuel** (1835–1902) English writer and intellectual controversialist: "What could be subtler,/ than the thought of Sam Butler?"

**Calverley, C. S.** (1831–1884) English barrister and writer of light verse, including a defense of tobacco 150 years early.

**Camuti, Louis J.,** (1893–1981) and **Lloyd Alexander** (1924– ) Camuti was for many years a veterinarian in New York City, known for treating cats (to which he was allergic); he wrote *Park Avenue Vet* with Alexander's assistance. Another of his books was called *All My Patients Are Under the Bed*.

**Čapek, Karel** (1890–1938) Czech essayist, journalist, and successful playwright.

**Caras, Roger** (1928– ) American writer and broadcaster, author of numerous books on animals and animal behavior.

**Carroll, Lewis** (1832–1898) Author of *Alice in Wonderland*.

**Casanova, Giacomo** (1725–1798) Writer and librarian.

**Cellini, Benvenuto** (1500–1571) Italian sculptor and autobiographer.

**Chandler, Raymond** (1888–1959) English-born author of tough-guy Los Angeles novels.

**Chateaubriand, François René, vicomte de** (1768–1848) Writer, refugee from the French Revolution, major French Romantic.

**Chaucer, Geoffrey** (c. 1343–1400) The original great English writer, author of *The Canterbury Tales*.

**Chekhov, Anton** (1860–1904) Russian playwright and short story writer, doctor, and humanist.

**Churchill, Winston** (1874–1965) Wartime British leader, prolific author of memoirs and histories.

**Cicero** (106–43 b.c.) Most influential, if not necessarily the best, Roman prose writer. Executed as a result of speaking out against Mark Antony after Caesar's assassination.

**Clare, John** (1793–1864) An authentic countryman-poet whose work dealt honestly with rural themes; spent much of his life locked up, mad.

**Clark, Eleanor** (1913–1996) American writer of fiction and several brilliant travel books, including books on Rome and on a Brittany oyster village.

**Clinton, Bill** (1946– ) Forty-second president of the U.S. His cat, Socks, became a pet celebrity when the Clinton family moved into the White House.

**Colette** (1873–1954) French novelist, wonderfully vivid writer about childhood in provincial France among other subjects.

**Constant, Benjamin** (1767–1830) French novelist (best-known: *Adolphe*) and writer of political and religious treatises.

**Cope, Wendy** (1945– ) Acerbic English writer of light verse, including a volume entitled *Making Cocoa for Kingsley Amis*.

**Coppée, François** (1842–1908) French poet and dramatist.

**Coward, Noel** (1897–1973) Actor, playwright, lyricist, and author of many classic songs and plays between World War I and World War II.

**Cowper, William** (1731–1800) English poet possessed of a delicate psyche; insane or suicidally depressed for much of his life, yet responsible for many poems and letters displaying an attractive, intimate wit.

**Crabbe, George** (1754–1832) An anti-Romantic, writer of coolly observed narrative and descriptive verse about the more depressing aspects of life in country villages; best known for the tale of Peter Grimes, turned into an opera by Benjamin Britten.

**Dahlberg, Edward** (1907–1977) American poet and essayist.

**Darwin, Charles** (1809–1882) The great naturalist, author of *The Origin of Species*, and lifelong accumulator of interesting facts.

**Darwin, Erasmus** (1731–1802) The botanist-poet, author of (among other curious mixtures of science and verse) *The Loves of the Plants*. A "Darwinian" before his time.

**Davies, Robertson** (1913–1995) Canadian novelist, playwright, and essayist.

**Davies, W. H.** (1871–1940) Poet, author of *Autobiography of a Super-Tramp*.

**De Baïf, Jean-Antoine** (1532–1589) French courtier, poet, and member of the literary group known as the Pléiade.

**De Kock, Paul** (1793–1871) Author of dubious French novels.

**Deng Xiaoping** (1904–1997) Chinese leader and phrasemaker.

**Denham, Sidney** English bibliographer of books about cats.

**de Saint-Cyran, Abbé** (1581–1643) French priest.

**Devoe, Alan** (1909–1955) American naturalist and author of a number of books about animals, tame and wild.

**Dickens, Charles** (1812–1870) Greatly loved English novelist, the most popular writer of the Victorian era.

**Dickinson, Emily** (1830–1886) Elusive, retiring, quirky, fascinating American poet.

**Dobbin, Orlando** (1807–1890) English light versifier.

**Dumas, Alexandre** (1802–1870) Author of swashbuckling French historical novels (e.g., *The Three Musketeers*), known as Dumas père because his son Alexandre (Dumas fils) was also a writer.

**Einstein, Albert** (1879–1955) A genius whose understanding encompassed even cats.

**Eliot, George** (1819–1880) Pen name of Mary Ann Evans, author of several wonderful novels, including *Middlemarch*.

**Eliot, T. S.** (1888–1965) Powerful, gloomy American-born English poet, ironically famous now for one of his few unserious productions, *Old Possum's Book of Practical Cats*, source for the musical *Cats*.

**Emerson, Ralph Waldo** (1803–1882) The original Transcendentalist, purveyor of much gnomically expressed wisdom.

*Encyclopedia Britannica* Founded in Scotland in the late eighteenth century, the *Britannica* migrated first to London, then New York, and finally to Chicago, where it has been digitalized.

**Ewart, Gavin** (1916–1995) Skillful English writer of verse, mainly light.

**Fielding, Henry** (1707–1754) Original and entertaining popular writer, who did much to create the art of the novel. Lord Byron called him "the prose Homer of human nature."

**Fisher, Dorothy Canfield** (1879–1958) Down-home New England novelist.

**Flatman, Thomas** (1637–1688) Painter (of miniatures) and poet (specializing in death).

**Fleischer, Leonore** American journalist.

**Fodor, Jerry** (1935– ) Professor of philosophy and psychology at Rutgers University, author of *Concepts* and *In Critical Condition*.

**Fogle, Bruce** (1944– ) Veterinarian, author of a number of books on dog and cat care.

**Fuller, Thomas** (1654–1734) A physician who wrote, in addition to medical works, three collections of proverbs.

**Galton, Francis** (1822–1911) English scientist, founder of eugenics, cousin of Charles Darwin.

**Garnett, Richard** (1835–1906) Enormously erudite librarian at the British Museum, member of the large clan of literary Garnetts.

**Gautier, Theophile** (1811–1872) Critic and novelist with a long and prominent career as a Paris journalist.

**Gray, Sir Alexander** (1882–1868) Scottish economist and expert on ballads.

**Gray, Cecil** (1895–1941) English musicologist, biographer of the composer Peter Warlock.

**Gray, Thomas** (1716–1771) English poet, friend of Horace Walpole to whom he sent verses on the death of Walpole's cat in a goldfish bowl.

**Greenburg, Dan** (1936– ) Funny American writer, largely of fiction for children.

**Greer, Germaine** (1939– ) Australian-born English polemicist.

**Hammond, Celia** English newspaper columnist.

**Hardy, Thomas** (1840–1928) Largely pessimistic English novelist and poet.

**Hare, M. E.** (1886–1967) English writer.

**Hearn, Lafcadio** (1850–1904) American journalist who settled in Japan, married a Japanese wife, and wrote extensively about the country and its people.

**Hemingway, Ernest** (1899–1961) Novelist and short story writer, at his best in the latter.

**Herbert, George** (1593–1633) Clergyman and profoundly religious poet.

**Herford, Oliver** (1863–1935) Anglo-American poet, illustrator, and wit, author of dozens of books (many of them about cats), who in his heyday was called "the most quoted man in America."

**Herodotus** (c. 480–c. 425 b.c.) Greek historian.

**Herrick, Robert** (1591–1674) English priest and author of brilliant secular and religious poems, including some of the finest lyrics ever written.

**Hoagland, Edward** (1932– ) American writer, called by John Updike "the best essayist of my generation."

**Hoban, Russell** (1925– ) English novelist, best known for *Riddley Walker* and for many children's books.

**Hoffmann, E. T. A.** (1776–1822) German writer of fantastic stories, the subject of Offenbach's opera *Tales of Hoffmann*.

**Holland, Sir Henry** (1788–1872) Queen Victoria's doctor.

**Household, Geoffrey** (1900–1988) English writer of thrillers.

**Hudson, W. H.** (1841–1922) Author of wonderful books on natural history, including several on South America; his most famous book was *Green Mansions*.

**Hue, Jean-Louis** French animal physiologist, writer on cats.

**Hughes, Ted** (1930–1999) British Poet Laureate, author of many poems dealing with animals, birds, and the natural world.

**Hunt, Leigh** (1784–1859) English poet and journalist, satirized by Dickens for his fecklessness.

**Huxley, Aldous** (1894–1963) English satirical novelist and portentous thinker.

**Huxley, Maria** (1898–1955) Aldous Huxley's first wife.

**Huxley, T. H.** (1825–1895) Natural historian, immensely successful popularizer of science.

**Huysmans, Joris-Karl** (1848–1907) French novelist, proponent of fin de siècle decadence.

**Hywel Dda (Howel the Good)** Tenth-century ruler in South Wales best known for promulgating a set of laws.

**Inge, William Ralph** (1860–1954) English clergyman (dean of St. Paul's Cathedral) and writer on religious and mystical subjects; after he retired he contributed a regular column to the *London Evening Standard*.

**James, Henry** (1843–1916) The great novelist, who never displayed any strong affection for cats.

**James, P. D.** (1920– ) Author of the best modern detective novels.

**Jarrell, Randall** (1914–1965) Affecting poet and brilliant critic; like so many of his fellows, apparently committed suicide after succumbing to alcohol.

**Jerome, Jerome K.** (1859–1927) English humorous novelist, best known for *Three Men in a Boat*.

**Jerrer, Ludwig** Nineteenth-century American cat hater.

**Johnson, Samuel** (1709–1784) Lexicographer, critic, and masterly conversationalist.

**Joseph, Michael** English publisher who wrote several books about cats and published many others during the first half of the twentieth century.

**Joyce, James** (1882–1941) Irish author of *Ulysses* and *Finnegans Wake*.

**Keillor, Garrison** (1942– ) American writer and broadcaster, mainstay of *The Prairie Home Companion*.

**Kilvert, Francis** (1840–1879) English clergyman, author of wonderfully evocative diaries recording life in a parish on the Welsh border.

**Kingsley, Charles** (1819–1875) Middling novelist and poet, controversial central figure in nineteenth-century English intellectual life.

**Kipling, Rudyard** (1865–1936) The poet of empire.

**Kliban, B.** (1935– ) American writer, cartoonist, and bard of the cat.

**Krutch, Joseph Wood** (1893–1970) Drama critic, professor of English (at Columbia University) and author of several fine books on natural history.

**Kunstler, William** (1919–1995) Celebrated American criminal lawyer and controversialist.

**Labouchere, Henry** (1798–1869) British politician and statesman.

**Landor, Walter Savage** (1775–1864) Bad-tempered English poet and writer of "imaginary conversations."

**Lang, Andrew** (1844–1912) Scottish literary man who wrote everything from poetry to bibliographies and is now remembered mostly for his fairy-tale collections.

**Lear, Edward** (1812–1888) Sad author of funny nonsense rhymes.

**Lemaître, François Elie Jules** (1853–1914) French poet and dramatist.

**Leonard, Hugh** (1926– ) Irish playwright.

**Lessing, Doris** (1919– ) After growing up in what is now Zimbabwe, emigrated to England and became a highly regarded novelist.

**Lichtenberg, Georg Christoph** (1742–1799) German scientist, philosopher, and Anglophile.

**Lincoln, Abraham** (1809–1865) President and master prose stylist.

**Lindbergh, Anne Morrow** (1906– ) Wife of Charles Lindbergh, author of several elegantly written volumes of memoirs.

**Lodge, Thomas** (1558–1625) Poet and prose romancier.

**Lucas, E. V.** (1868–1938) Prolific journeyman writer of many books of travel, fiction, biography, and more.

**Mansfield, Katharine** (1888–1923) English short story writer, born in New Zealand. A bit of a case.

**Marquis, Don** (1878–1937) American journalist, author of the tales of Archy, the typewriting cockroach (who never used capital letters because he could hit only one key at a time), and Archy's friend Mehitabel the cat.

**McGough, Roger** (1937– ) Engaging English poet who came to the fore in the 1960s.

**Melville, Herman** (1819–1891) Great American novelist, author of *Moby-Dick*, embittered by the commercial failure of his books.

**Méry, François-Joseph** (1798–1865) French poet, satirist, prolific novelist, short story writer, and critic; author (with C. Du Locle) of the libretto of Verdi's opera *Don Carlos*.

**Meynell, Sir Francis** (1891–1975) Journalist and typographer, founder of the Nonesuch Press.

**Mikes, George** (1912–1987) Hungarian-born British writer.

**Mitchell, Henry** (1923–1993) One of the finest garden writers of our time, pointed and witty.

**Mitford, Nancy** (1904–1973) Entertaining and pungent novelist.

**Mivart, St. George** (1827–1900) Biologist, author of the first comprehensive scientific study of the cat; a Catholic convert, he managed to get himself excommunicated late in life by writing articles challenging church authority.

**Moncrif, François Auguste Paradis de** (1687–1770) Courtier to Louis XV, remembered mainly for his love of cats and his book *Lettres sur les Chats*.

**Montaigne, Michel de** (1533–1592) The insatiably curious and humane essayist.

**Morgan, Henry** (1915–1994) Television actor and comedian.

**Morris, Desmond** (1928– ) Best-selling writer on animal and human behavior (*The Naked Ape*, *Manwatching*, *Dogwatching*, etc.).

**Munro, H. H.** ("Saki") (1870–1916) Writer of short stories, mostly macabre, and political satire. Killed at the front in World War I.

**Nash, Ogden** (1902–1971) Unmetrical American poet.

***New England Primer,*** The famous American schoolbook, first published before 1690. An estimated two million copies sold during the eighteenth century.

**Nichols, Beverley** (1899–1983) Prolific English writer of whimsical gardening books and much journalism.

*Oologist Magazine,* The magazine for collectors of birds' eggs, long since defunct.

**O'Rourke, P. J.** (1946– ) Savage if sometimes inconsistent American political writer.

**Paglia, Camille** (1947– ) Outspoken American postfeminist.

**Phelps, William Lyon** (1865–1943) Literary enthusiast responsible for a fairly large bookshelf full of essays, criticism, and miscellaneous writings.

**Pirinçci, Akif** (1959– ) and **Degen, Rolf** Joint authors of a highly regarded German book on cat physiology and behavior.

**Pope, Alexander** (1688–1774) Poet and satirist.

**Potter, Beatrix** (1866–1943) The author of *Peter Rabbit* and other major works; she wrote her journal in code that wasn't deciphered until many years after her death.

**Ransome, Arthur** (1884–1967) Journalist and writer, particularly memorable for his *Swallows and Amazons* books for children. Great fishing writer, too.

**Raverat, Gwen** (1885–1957) English artist and granddaughter of Charles Darwin. Her charming memoir *Period Piece* describes growing up in Cambridge, England, a hundred years ago.

**Ray, John** (1627–1705) England's first great naturalist. He also compiled a book of proverbs.

**Repplier, Agnes** (1858–1950) Philadelphia essayist; she wrote biographies, collections of essays, and at least two books on cats: *The Cat* and *The Fireside Sphinx*, a cat anthology.

**Rimsky-Korsakov, Nikolai** (1844–1908) Russian composer.

**Robinson, Louis** Nineteenth-century English naturalist.

**Roethke, Theodore** (1908–1963) American poet and professor, writer of knotty verse and also delightful nonsense.

**Ronsard, Pierre** (1524–1585) French lyric poet and confirmed cat hater.

**Runyon, Damon** (1884–1946) New York journalist and specialist in odd characters (*Guys and Dolls*).

**Saint-Saëns, Camille** (1835–1921) French composer.

**Salmon, William** (1644–1713) English doctor, possibly a quack, author of numerous books including a complete medical guide for home use.

**Salten, Felix** (1869–1945) Austrian author of many animal stories, among them most notably *Bambi*.

**Sarton, May** (1912–1995) American poet and novelist.

**Savage, Eliza Mary Anne** Cat-obsessed correspondent of Samuel Butler (q.v.), described by Van Vechten as "equally eccentric."

**Schafer, Murray** (1933– ) Canadian writer and avant-garde composer with an interest in what he calls "the soundscape."

**Schopenhauer, Arthur** (1788–1860) German philosopher.

**Scott, Sir Walter** (1771–1832) Hardworking Scottish novelist.

**Sei Shōnagon** Tenth-century Japanese court lady, author of a wonderful book of observations and thoughts, *The Pillow Book*.

**Service, William** (1930– ) Author of only one small but almost perfect book about adopting and raising an owl (in a house with a cat).

**Shakespeare, William** (1564–1616) The playwright.

**Sidney, Sir Philip** (1554–86) English poet and ideal gentleman.

**Skelton, John** (1460?–1529) One-time tutor to Henry VIII, vigorous poet, inventor of the quick doggerel known as "skeltonic verse."

**Smart, Christopher** (1722–1771) Mad or half-mad much of his life, a powerful and original poet nonetheless.

**Smith, Stevie** (1902–1971) Minor English novelist better known for her quirky, sharp-tongued verse.

**Snyder, Gary** (1930– ) Beat Generation poet with an affinity for Oriental verse forms and subject matter.

**Southey, Robert** (1774–1843) English poet whose copious output never reached the top rank.

*Spectator,* The periodical conducted by Richard Steele and Joseph Addison for a few years between 1711 and 1714.

**Spencer, Stanley** (1891–1959) English painter.

**Stafford, Jean** (1915–1979) American novelist and short story writer.

**Steele, Richard** (1672–1729) English essayist, playwright, editor, and pamphleteer.

**Stevenson, Anne** (1933– ) Fine American poet who now lives in England.

**Stevenson, Robert Louis** (1850–1894) Scottish novelist (*Treasure Island*, *Kidnapped*, etc.) who ended up for reasons of health in Samoa but nevertheless died there, too young.

**Strachey, Julia** (1901–1979) English novelist and short story writer.

**Strachey, Lytton** (1880–1932) Essayist, destructive biographer, man of letters.

**Swift, Jonathan** (1667–1745) Irish satirist and wonderfully lively and readable poet, unlikely Dean of St. Patrick's in Dublin. "Cousin Swift, you will never be a poet," Dryden is supposed to have told him.

**Swinnerton, Frank** (1884–1982) Amazingly long-lived and productive English novelist and critic.

**Taine, Hippolyte** (1828–1893) French polymath, philosopher, historian, and critic.

**Tangye, Derek** British writer who produced several books about various cats he had owned.

**Tennyson, Alfred Lord** (1809–1892) The preeminent poet of Victorian England, Poet Laureate for more than forty years.

**Tessimond, A. J.** (1902–1962) English writer.

**Theocritus** (c. 308–c. 240 b.c.) Greek pastoral poet.

**Thomas, Elizabeth Marshall** (1931– ) American ethologist, author of fascinating books on dogs and cats.

**Thoreau, Henry David** (1817–1862) Another Concord mystic, with a wonderfully unmystical, precise, interested approach to writing about the natural world—and himself.

**Thurber, James** (1894–1961) American writer of extremely funny, unforced humor. Also drew memorable cartoons.

**Tickner, John** English writer and cartoonist.

**Topsell, Edward** (died 1638?) Churchman and author of often amusing books on "four-footed beastes" and snakes.

**Turberville, George** (1540?-1610?) Elizabethan poet and translator.

**Twain, Mark** (1835–1910) Pen name of Samuel Clemens, American humorist.

**Unamuno, Miguel de** (1864–1936) Spanish writer and philosopher (*The Tragic Sense of Life*).

**Underhill, Evelyn** (1875–1941) English writer and cat lover; in her Who's Who entry she listed among her recreations "talking to cats."

**Updike, John** (1932– ) One of the finest novelists of our time, and also an accomplished writer of (mainly) light verse.

**Van Vechten, Carl** (1880–1964) American author of one of the best of all cat books, *The Tiger in the House*, as well as novels and criticism; he played a role in encouraging and publicizing the Harlem Renaissance of the 1920s.

**Veblen, Thorstein** (1857–1929) The apostle of "conspicuous consumption."

**Warner, Charles Dudley** (1829–1900) American newspaper journalist and author of the charming *My Summer in a Garden*.

**Warner, Sylvia Townsend** (1893–1978) English novelist and poet who frequently expressed her dislike of cats—but wrote about them with perceptiveness.

**Webster, Noah** (1758–1843) American lexicographer.

**Wells, H. G.** (1866–1946) Novelist and futurologist.

**White, Gilbert** (1720–1993) Curate of Selborne in Hampshire, where he was born and spent his whole life, closely observing the natural world around him and writing about it in his incomparable journals.

**White, T. H.** (1906–1964) English writer and naturallist.

**Whitehead, Alfred North** (1861–1947) British mathematician and philosopher.

**Whittier, John Greenleaf** (1807–1892)
Patriotic New England poet.

**Will, George F.** (1941– ) American journalist.

**Williams, William Carlos** (1883–1963) Liberal
American poet and doctor.

**Wodehouse, P. G.** (1881–1975) Prolific English
fiction writer, known for his comic genius.

**Woolf, Virginia** (1882–1941) Innovative
though not always exciting English novelist,
delightful critic.

**Yeats, William Butler** (1865–1939) Splendid
Irish poet.

**Zola, Emile** (1840–1902) French novelist.

# INDEX

# ACKNOWLEDGMENTS

Elizabeth Bishop: "Lullaby for the Cat" from THE COMPLETE POEMS 1927–1979 by Elizabeth Bishop. Copyright © 1979, 1983 by Alice Helen Methfessel. Reprinted by permission of Farrar, Straus and Giroux, LLC.

Roger Caras: Excerpts reprinted with the permission of Simon & Schuster from A CAT IS WATCHING by Roger Caras. Copyright © 1989 by Roger Caras.

Wendy Cope: "An Unusual Cat Poem" reprinted by permission of Sterling Lord Literistic, Inc. Copyright © by Wendy Cope.

T. S. Eliot: Excerpt from "Macavity: The Mystery Cat" in OLD POSSUM'S BOOK OF PRACTICAL CATS, copyright 1939 by T. S. Eliot and renewed 1967 by Esme Valerie Eliot, reprinted by permission of Harcourt, Inc.

Don Marquis: From ARCHY'S LIFE OF MEHITABEL by Don Marquis. Copyright 1927, 1933 by Doubleday, a divison of Random House, Inc. Used by permission of Doubleday, a division of Random House, Inc.

Roger McGough: Reprinted by permission of The Peters Fraser and Dunlop Group Limited on behalf of Roger McGough © 1989.

Desmond Morris: Reprinted by permission of Crown Publishers from CATLORE copyright © 1986 by Desmond Morris and CATWATCHING copyright © 1987 by Desmond Morris.

Ogden Nash: From VERSES FROM 1929 ON by Ogden Nash. Copyright © 1940 by Ogden Nash; first appeared in SATURDAY EVENING POST. By permission of Little, Brown and Company (Inc.).

Akif Pirinçci and Rolf Degen: Excerpt from DAS GROSSE FELIDAE KATZENBUCH by Akif Pirinçci and Rolf Degen copyright © 1994 Wilhelm Goldmann Verlag within Verlagsgruppe Bertelsmann